# Objective-C Quick
# Syntax Reference

Matthew Campbell

Apress®

## Objective-C Quick Syntax Reference

ISBN-13 (pbk): 978-1-4302-6487-3

ISBN-13 (electronic): 978-1-4302-6488-0

President and Publisher: Paul Manning
Lead Editor: Steve Anglin
Technical Reviewer: Charles Cruz
Editorial Board: Steve Anglin, Mark Beckner, Ewan Buckingham, Gary Cornell, Louise Corrigan, Jonathan Gennick, James DeWolf Jonathan Hassell, Robert Hutchinson, Michelle Lowman, James Markham, Matthew Moodie, Jeff Olson, Jeffrey Pepper, Douglas Pundick, Ben Renow-Clarke, Dominic Shakeshaft, Gwenan Spearing, Steve Weiss, Tom Welsh
Coordinating Editor: Anamika Panchoo
Copy Editor: Mary Behr
Compositor: SPi Global
Indexer: SPi Global
Artist: SPi Global
Cover Designer: Anna Ishchenko

Distributed to the book trade worldwide by Springer Science+Business Media New York, 233 Spring Street, 6th Floor, New York, NY 10013. Phone 1-800-SPRINGER, fax (201) 348-4505, e-mail orders-ny@springer-sbm.com, or visit www.springeronline.com. Apress Media, LLC is a California LLC and the sole member (owner) is Springer Science + Business Media Finance Inc (SSBM Finance Inc). SSBM Finance Inc is a Delaware corporation.

For information on translations, please e-mail rights@apress.com, or visit www.apress.com.

Apress and friends of ED books may be purchased in bulk for academic, corporate, or promotional use. eBook versions and licenses are also available for most titles. For more information, reference our Special Bulk Sales–eBook Licensing web page at www.apress.com/bulk-sales.

Any source code or other supplementary materials referenced by the author in this text is available to readers at www.apress.com. For detailed information about how to locate your book's source code, go to www.apress.com/source-code/.

*For my daughter, Keira*

# Contents at a Glance

# Contents

# About the Author

**Matthew Campbell** is a professional software developer, entrepreneur, author, and trainer. He works for Mobile App Mastery, a web-based software development training company he founded in 2008. Before building Mobile App Mastery, Matt studied psychology, worked as a mental health counselor, and supported psychometric research as a data analyst at the Educational Testing Service in Princeton. The books and trainings that he creates are designed to remove the obstacles that stop developers from mastering their craft.

# About the Technical Reviewer

**Charles Cruz** is a mobile application developer for the iOS, Android, and Windows Phone platforms. He graduated from Stanford University with B.S. and M.S. degrees in engineering. He lives in Southern California and runs a photography business with his wife (www.facebook.com/BellaLenteStudios). When not doing technical things, he plays lead guitar in an original metal band (www.taintedsociety.com). Charles can be reached at codingandpicking@gmail.com and @CodingNPicking on Twitter.

# Introduction

Objective-C is a tool that you can use to create stunning applications for the Mac, iPhone, and iPad. This unique programming language traces its linage back to the C programming language. Objective-C is C with object-oriented programming.

Today, learning programming is about learning how to shape our world. Objective-C programmers are in a unique position to create mobile applications that people all over the world can use in their daily lives.

Objective-C is a delight to use. While other programming languages can feel clumsy at times, Objective-C will show you its power and reach with grace. Problems that seem intractable in other programming languages melt away in Objective-C.

At its core, this book is about laying out, without any fuss, what Objective-C can do. When you know what you want to do, but you just need to know the Objective-C way to do it, use this book to get help.

# CHAPTER 1

# Hello World

## Xcode

Objective-C is a programming language that extends the C programming language to include object-oriented programming capabilities. This means that most classic C programming procedures are used in Objective-C programs. For the purposes of this book, you will need to have an idea of how C programming works.

Before you write any Objective-C code, you will need to have the proper tool for the job. For Objective-C, this tool is Xcode. Xcode will be your primary code editor and integrated development environment (IDE).

---

**Note**   Xcode requires a Mac. You cannot install Xcode on a Windows-or Linux-based computer.

---

To install Xcode, go to the Mac App Store by selecting your Mac's menu bar and then choosing  ➤ **App Store**. Use the App Store search feature to locate Xcode by typing the word **Xcode** into the textbox next to the hourglass. Press return to search for Xcode. You will be presented with a list of apps, and Xcode should be the first app in the list. Install Xcode by clicking the button with the word **free** next to the Xcode icon. See Figure 1-1 for the screen that you should see once you searched for Xcode in the App Store.

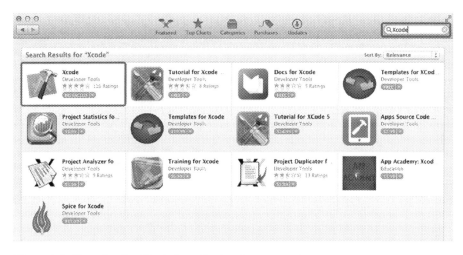

*Figure 1-1.  Downloading Xcode from the App Store*

# Creating a New Project

Open Xcode by going to your **Applications** folder and clicking the Xcode app. You will be presented with a welcome screen that includes text that reads **Create a new Xcode project** (see Figure 1-2). Click the text **Create a new Xcode project** to get started.

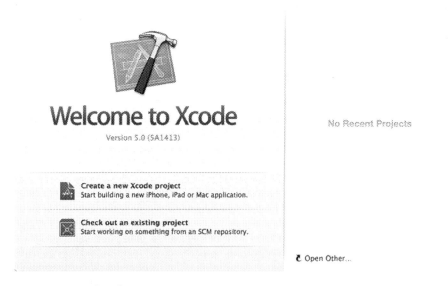

*Figure 1-2.  Xcode welcome screen*

The next screen that appears will list options for creating apps both for iOS and Mac. In this book, you will be using a Mac Command Line Tool app, so set up this by choosing **OSX ➤ Application ➤ Command Line Tool**.

When the next screen appears, just give your new project a name, choose the type Foundation, leave the other settings as they are, and then click **Next**.

Now choose a folder to save the Xcode project on your Mac. Once you do this, an Xcode screen will appear. The Xcode screen will include a list of files on the left and a code editor in the center (see Figure 1-3).

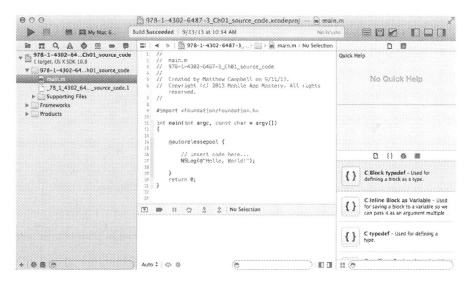

*Figure 1-3.*  *Code editor and project navigator*

# Hello World

Writing Hello World in code is what we do when want to make sure that we have set up a code project correctly. Xcode makes this really easy to do because new Command Line Tool projects come with Hello World already coded.

All you need to do is use the **Project Navigator**, the widget on the left-hand area of your Xcode screen, to locate the file named **main.m**. Click **main.m** to open the file in the code editor (Figure 1-4).

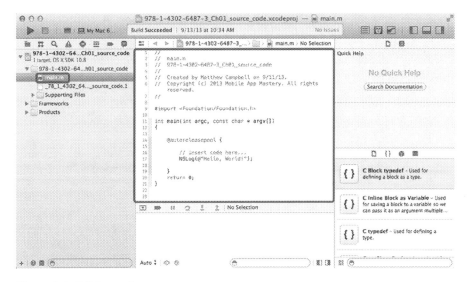

***Figure 1-4.*** *Editing main.m*

When you do this you will see code that looks a bit like this:

```
#import <Foundation/Foundation.h>

int main(int argc, const char * argv[]){
    @autoreleasepool {
        // insert code here...
        NSLog(@"Hello, World!");
    }
    return 0;
}
```

Much of the code above sets up the application, starting with the `#import` statement. This statement imports the code that you need, called **Foundation**, for your Objective-C program to work.

The next part of the code above is the function named `main`, which contains all the program code and returns the integer 0 when the program is complete.

Inside the main function you will see an Objective-C auto release pool. Auto release pools are required to support the memory management system used with Objective-C. The auto release pool is declared with the `@autoreleasepool` keyword.

In the middle of all this code, you can see the Hello World code, which looks like this:

```
NSLog(@"Hello, World!");
```

The first piece of this is the function `NSLog`. `NSLog` is used to write messages to the console log. Xcode's console log is located at the bottom of the Xcode screen (Figure 1-5) and presents error messages along with messages that you send using `NSLog`.

4

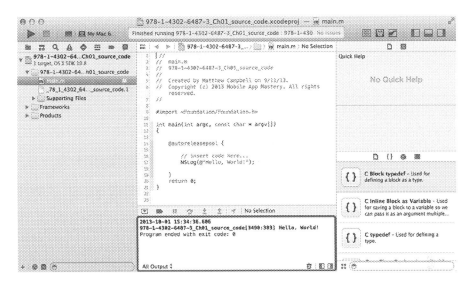

***Figure 1-5.*** *Hello World output in console screen*

---

▒ **Note** By default the console log is hidden along with the debugger at the bottom of the screen. To see these two components you must unhide the bottom screen by clicking the **Hide or Show Debug Area** toggle located in the top right-hand part of the Xcode screen. This button is located in the middle of a set of three buttons.

---

The string Hello World is enclosed with quotes ("") and the Objective-C escape character @. The @ character is used in Objective-C to let the compiler know that certain keywords or code have special Objective-C properties. When @ is before a string in double quotes, as in @"Hello, World!", it means that the string is an Objective-C NSString object.

# Code Comments

There is one more line of code that Xcode helpfully inserted into this project for you. This line of code is a good example of a code comment and begins with these two special characters: //. Here is what the code comment looks like:

```
// insert code here...
```

Code comments are used to help document your code by giving you a way to insert text into the program that will not be compiled into a working program.

# Build and Run

To test the code, click the Run button in the top upper left area of the Xcode screen. See Figure 1-6 to see which button to push.

When you click the Run button, Xcode will compile the code in the Xcode project and then run the program. The program you have been working on will print out the words Hello World. You can see the output circled in Figure 1-6.

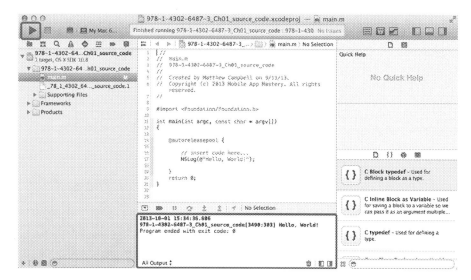

***Figure 1-6.*** *Building and running the Hello World code*

# Where to Get More Information

This book is a quick reference for Objective-C, and I have focused on the code and patterns that I judge will be most useful for most people. However, this means that I can't include everything in this book.

The best place to get complete information on Objective-C and the Mac and iOS applications that you can create with Objective-C is the Apple Developer web site. You can get to the Apple Developer web site by using a web browser to navigate to http://developer.apple.com/resources.

This web site contains guides, source code, and code documentation. The part of the web site that will be most relevant to the topics in this book is the code documentation for the Foundation framework. You can use the web site's search features to look for a specific class like NSObject, or you can search for the word Foundation or Objective-C.

**CHAPTER 2**

# Build and Run

## Compiling

Objective-C code needs to be turned into machine code that runs on an iOS device or a Mac. This process is called compiling, and Xcode uses the LLVM compiler to create machine code. Xcode templates used to create new projects, like you did in Chapter 1, will have the settings that the compiler needs to set this up for you.

## Building

Compiling code is usually only part of the process involved with creating an app. Apps destined to be distributed to Mac and iPhone users require other resources in addition to the compiled code. This includes content like pictures, movies, music, and databases.

These resources, along with an app directory structure, are all packed into a special file called a **Bundle**. You will use Xcode to compile your source code and then package everything into the bundle that you need for you app. This process is called **Building** in Xcode.

If you look under the **Project** menu item in your Xcode menu bar (Figure 2-1), you will see options for building your program. Usually you will just use the **Build and Run** feature of Xcode to creating compile and test your code.

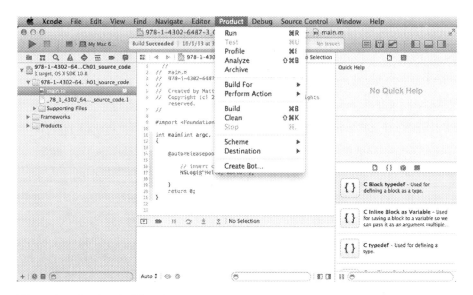

*Figure 2-1.* *Product build options*

# Build and Run

Use the **Build and Run** button (see Figure 2-2) located in the upper left-hand area of your Xcode screen (this is an arrow that looks like a play button) to build your app.

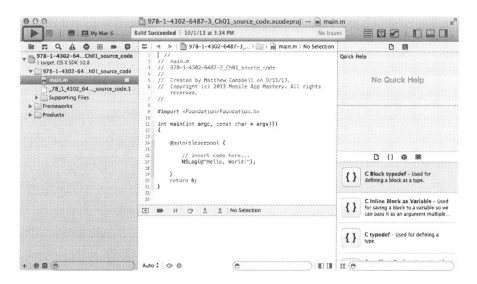

*Figure 2-2.* *Build and Run button*

Xcode will not only build your app, but execute the code as well. If you click the Build and Run button for the current program, you should see the following text appear in your console log (also shown in Figure 2-3):

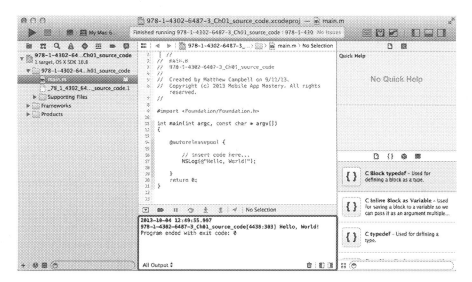

***Figure 2-3.*** *Console log's Hello World output*

```
2014-01-12 06:22:48.382
Ch01_source_code[13018:303] Hello, World!
Program ended with exit code: 0
```

Your output won't match mine exactly, but you should see the words **Hello World!** and the name of your project on the screen.

---

▓ **Note** While most apps will get a bundle along with the compiled machine code included, I don't need that for the apps I am using to demonstrate the code used in this book. If you locate your compiled code file, you will only find one Unix Executable File that you can run with the Mac Terminal app.

---

# CHAPTER 3

# Variables

## Variables Defined

Objective-C stores information in variables. These are divided into two types: primitive types and composite types. Primitive variables store one piece of information, such as a number or a character. Composite variables store a set of information, such as three related numbers and a character.

### Data Types

Table 3-1 shows the most common primitive data types that you will see in Objective-C.

*Table 3-1. Objective-C Data Types*

| Data Type | Format Specifier | Description |
| --- | --- | --- |
| NSInteger | %li | Signed integer |
| NSUInteger | %lu | Unsigned integer |
| BOOL | %i | Boolean (YES/NO) |
| CGFloat | %f | Floating point |

**Note** Objective-C programs can use C data types like int, long, float, double, and char in addition to the Objective-C data types listed in Table 3-1. This is because Objective-C is based on the C programming language and so inherits all of C's functionality in addition to the Objective-C syntax that we are discussing here.

## Declaring Variables

Variables are declared in Objective-C with their data type first, followed by a variable name. You must declare a variable before using it. Variable names should be meaningful, but you can name a variable anything that you want.

Here is how you would declare an integer in Objective-C:

```
NSUInteger numberOfPeople;
```

## Assigning Values

You can use the assignment operator (=) to assign a value to a variable, like so:

```
numberOfPeople = 100;
```

Once you have assigned a value, you can retrieve and use that value by referencing the variable name.

```
NSLog(@"The number of people is %lu", numberOfPeople);
```

---

▓ **Note**    You may have noticed that the NSLog statement required the %lu symbol. This symbol is called a format specifier and NSLog will use it as a placeholder to insert values in the comma-separated list that appears right after the string. See Table 3-1 for a list of the format specifiers that you must use with Objective-C data types.

---

You can also declare variables and assign values on the same line if you like.

```
NSUInteger numberOfGroups = 20;
```

## Integer Types

Integers are whole numbers, so any number that doesn't need a decimal point is an integer. In Objective-C, integers are expressed with the data types NSInteger and NSUInteger.

NSUIntegers are unsigned integers, which means that they can only be positive numbers. The maximum value that an NSUInteger can take depends on the system for which the Objective-C code is compiled. If you compile for a 64-bit Mac, the maximum value will be 18,446,744,073,709,551,615.

For 32-bit platforms like the iPhone 5 and below, the maximum value is 4,294,967,295. You can check these numbers yourself using the NSUIntegerMax constant.

```
NSLog(@"NSUIntegerMax is %lu", NSUIntegerMax);
```

NSIntegers are signed integers, which means that they can be either positive or negative. The maximum value of an NSInteger is half of the NSUInteger value because NSInteger must support both positive and negative numbers.

So, if you need huge numbers, you may need to stick to NSUInteger, but if you need to handle both positive and negative numbers, you will need NSInteger. You can check the minimum and maximum value of NSInteger on your system with the NSIntegerMin and NSIntegerMax constants.

```
NSLog(@"NSIntegerMin is %li", NSIntegerMin);
NSLog(@"NSIntegerMax is %li", NSIntegerMax);
```

# Boolean Types

Boolean date types are used when values can either be true or false. In Objective-C, this data type is declared as a BOOL type. BOOL types have values that are either YES or NO.

```
BOOL success = YES;
```

Since Objective-C stores BOOL values as 1 for YES and 0 for NO, you must use the %i format specifier print out a BOOL value. %i is another format specifier for integers.

```
NSLog(@"success is %i", success);
```

The NSLog statement above will print out 1 for YES and 0 for NO, but some people prefer to see the YES or NO strings printed out to the log. You can do so using this alternate statement:

```
NSLog(@"success: %@", success ? @"YES" : @"NO");
```

Here the variable success was replaced with a statement that has to be evaluated. This statement will return either the string YES or the string NO depending on the value of the variable success. If success is zero, then whatever is in the last position of the statement is returned, and if success is any other value then whatever is in the first position is returned. The ternary operator (?) tells the compiler to evaluate the statement.

# Float Types

Float types are represented in Objective-C with the CGFloat data type. CGFloat is what you use when you want decimal places in your number. For example, if you want to represent a percent, you may do something like this:

```
CGFloat percent = 33.34;
```

You can find the maximum value of CGFloat values for 32-bit systems using FLT_MAX. For 64-bit systems you must use DBL_MAX.

# Scope

Like most programming languages that trace their history back to C, Objective-C variables have their scope determined by the placement of these curly brackets, { }. When you enclose lines of code in { }, you are defining a block of code. Variables placed inside a block of code can only be used from inside that block of code. This is called scope.

For example, let's take the previous example that declared an unsigned integer called numberOfPeople, assigned a value to this variable, and then printed this value out to the log.

```
NSInteger numberOfPeople;
numberOfPeople = 100;
NSLog(@"The number of people is %li", numberOfPeople);
```

This code works perfectly fine because the variable numberOfPeople remains in scope the entire time you need it to. But if you use curly brackets to enclose the first two lines of code in their own region, the variable will work when you assign the value but not when you attempt to write out the value to the log. You will not be able to compile your program if you try to write out numberOfPeople to the log outside of the scope defined by the curly brackets.

```
{
    NSInteger numberOfPeople;
    numberOfPeople = 100;
}
NSLog(@"The number of people is %li", numberOfPeople);
```

Scope is used to define blocks of code for functions, loops, methods, if-statements and switch statements. All of these things are discussed later in this book.

# CHAPTER 4

# Operators

## Operators Defined

Operators are used to perform operations on values. You can do arithmetic, assignment, logical, and relational operations with operators.

### Arithmetic Operators

Arithmetic operators are used to perform math on values. You can use arithmetic operators to perform addition, subtraction, multiplication, division, and modulus (the remainder from a division operation). Table 4-1 lists Objective-C's arithmetic operators.

*Table 4-1.* *Arithmetic Operators*

| Operator | Meaning |
| --- | --- |
| + | Addition |
| - | Subtraction |
| * | Multiplication |
| / | Division |
| % | Modulus |

An operation will look like a math problem.

```
1.0 + 2.0 - 3.0 * 4.0 / 5.0;
```

The result from the line of code above won't do much because the result isn't being stored or used in a function. You can use the results of an operation immediately in a function like:

```
NSLog(@"1.0 + 2.0 - 3.0 * 4.0 / 5.0 = %f", 1.0 + 2.0 - 3.0 * 4.0 / 5.0);
```

You can also use an assignment operator to store the result in a variable to be used later on.

```
CGFloat t2 = 1.0 + 2.0 - 3.0 * 4.0 / 5.0;
```

You may notice that floating point numbers are used in the operations above. Each number in the expression has a decimal point and zero, and the t2 variable data type is CGFloat. This was deliberate because I suspected that the operation would result in a fractional number, requiring a floating point variable to be represented correctly.

---

▓ **Note**   Using the correct data types is essential when doing arithmetic operations, and the compiler will assume that any number without a decimal place is an integer. Operations involving only integers will return integers, which means that the result will be rounded. This could easily lead to unexpected results in your calculations.

---

## Operator Precedence

Operators are evaluated from left to right. Multiplication, division, and modulus operators are evaluated before addition and subtraction operators. If you want to change the order that operators are evaluated, you can enclose parts of the expression in parentheses. Doing this will change the results of your expressions, as shown:

```
NSLog(@"%f", 1.0 + 2.0 - 3.0 * 4.0 / 5.0);     // 0.600000
NSLog(@"%f", 1.0 + (2.0 - 3.0 * 4.0) / 5.0);   // -1.000000
NSLog(@"%f", (1.0 + 2.0 - 3.0 * 4.0) / 5.0);   // -1.800000
```

## Assignment Operators

The assignment operator (=) is used to assign a value to a variable. You can assign a value or the results of an operation to a variable using the assignment operator.

```
NSUInteger t2 = 100;
NSUInteger t3 = 10 * 10;
```

## Increment and Decrement Operators

You can combine the addition and subtraction operators with the assignment operator as a shortcut. Add a ++ to the variable name and the value will be incremented by 1 and automatically assigned to the variable.

```
t2++;
```

The line of code above will increment t2 by 1, making the value of t2 equal to 101. The following is the longer way of doing the same thing:

```
t2 = t2 + 1;
```

You can also reduce the value of t2 by adding the decrement operator (--) to the variable name.

```
t2--;
```

# Relational Operators

Relational operators are used to evaluate the relationship between two values. When you use relational operators, the result will be a BOOL data type. You can evaluate whether two values are the same or different. See Table 4-2 for a list of the available relational operators.

*Table 4-2.* *Relational Operators*

| Operator | Meaning |
| --- | --- |
| == | Equal to |
| != | Not equal to |
| > | Greater than |
| < | Less than |
| >= | Greater than or equal to |
| <= | Less than or equal to |

Here is an example of how to use a relational operator:

```
BOOL t4 = 5 < 4;
NSLog(@"t4 = %@", t4 ? @"YES" : @"NO"); // NO
```

This case seems trivial, but when you have variables whose values you don't know beforehand, evaluating relational operators is important. Relational operators are also used in if statements, which are a key programming tool. If statements are covered later.

# Logical Operators

Logical operators are used when you are evaluating more than one relationship between entities. These operators are used with the relational operators and they also return a BOOL result.

See Table 4-3 for a list of available logical operators.

*Table 4-3.* *Logical Operators*

| Operator | Meaning |
|----------|---------|
| && | AND |
| \|\| | OR |
| ! | NOT (Reverse result) |

Here's an example of how to use the logical operators:

```
BOOL t5 = YES && NO;        // NO
BOOL t6 = YES && YES;       // YES
BOOL t7 = YES || NO;        // YES
BOOL t8 = NO || NO;         // NO
BOOL t9 = !YES;             // NO
```

# CHAPTER 5

# Objects

## Objects Defined

Objective-C objects are entities that contain both behavior and attributes in one place. Behaviors are coded in methods while attributes are coded in properties. Objects can also include private instance variables. Private instance variables are used when data storage is required, but not needed to be shared.

### NSObject Class

NSObject is the root class in Objective-C. A class is a definition that has all the code needed to make an object's methods and properties work. NSObject is called the root class because it has all the code needed to make objects work in Objective-C and every other class inherits from the NSObject class.

### Object Declaration

A class is used like a data type. Data types are used to declare a variable and you have many variables for each data type. A class is used to declare an object and you can have one class with many objects.

Here is how you would declare an NSObject object:

```
NSObject object;
```

### Object Constructors

While data type variables can just be assigned to a value, objects require functions called constructors. Constructors assign memory resources to the object and do any setup that the object needs to function. Usually, you will see constructors split up into two functions called alloc and init.

```
object = [[NSObject alloc] init];
```

The init function will sometimes have a different name, but it will usually start with the letters init. For example, here is a constructor for an NSURL object that will point to my web site:

```
NSURL *url = [[NSURL alloc] initWithString:@"https://mobileappmastery.com"];
```

Notice that instead of init you have initWithString:. There aren't any rules, other than convention, when it comes to names of constructors.

While the pattern of alloc and init is the most common, you will also see object creation with other function names and with the new keyword.

```
NSDate *today = [NSDate date];
NSObject *object2 = [NSObject new];
```

While the new constructor is uncommon, the new keyword can be used in place of alloc and init. Constructors other than new, alloc, and init are used for temporary objects. The date object above is an example of an object that is used on a temporary basis because you usually just want to get a timestamp and move on. There is no reason to maintain an object like this for a long time.

---

▓ **Note** Temporary objects like the date object in the example are used more often in projects where ARC is not being used for memory management. ARC, or Automatic Reference Counting, is a system that manages each object's memory requirements. Projects built with ARC use temporary objects like the date object above when functionality is needed, but the object doesn't need to be maintained for any length of time.

---

## Object Format Specifier

When you want to use NSLog to print out data type values you must use a format specifier like %lu, %li, %f, or %i. The value gets substituted into the NSLog string, giving you a way to observe variable values. You can do this with objects as well.

NSObject objects and every object that derives from NSObject use the %@ format specifier. The output you get from NSLog depends on the type of object. If you print out the object from the example above like this

```
NSLog(@"object = %@", object);
```

you will get output that gives you details about the object including the class name and memory address.

```
object = <NSObject: 0x10010a0c0>
```

Other objects will report back more specific information; what gets reported back depends on the type of object. If you tried the same trick with the url NSURL object like this

```
NSLog(@"website = %@", url);
```

the console would present a listing of the web site URL.

```
website = https://mobileappmastery.com
```

# Messages

When you want an object to do something, you send a message to the object. Sending a message directs the object to execute the method defined in the class that corresponds to the message.

For instance, you could remove a file from your shared directory by sending a message to an NSFileManager object.

```
NSFileManager *fileManager = [NSFileManager defaultManager];
[fileManager removeItemAtPath:@"/Users/Shared/studyreport.txt"
                                            error:nil];
```

The first line of code above is declaring an NSFileManager object named fileManager. In the second line of code, you can see the example of the message being sent. The message is removeItemAtPath:error: and you send this message by writing this out and including the parameters (here, these are the item to remove and an optional error object). All of this is enclosed in square brackets, [ ], and ends with a semi-colon.

If you were to look at the class definition in the header file for NSFileManager, you would find the declaration for this method:

```
- (BOOL)removeItemAtPath:(NSString *)path error:(NSError **)error;
```

This method returns a BOOL value that you are not using here.

# CHAPTER 6

# Strings

## NSString

NSString is the class used in Objective-C to work with strings. NSString manages the list of characters that forms a string. NSString objects are immutable, which means that once you create an NSString object you can't change it.

NSString objects can be created with many different constructors, but the most common way you'll see NSString objects created is with the @ symbol followed by quotes. In fact, you've seen this already in the Hello World example from Chapter 1.

```
NSLog(@"Hello, World!");
```

That parameter is an NSString object, although it's hard to see since you don't need the explicit NSString declaration here. More often you will see NSString objects created like this:

```
NSString *firstName = @"Matthew";
NSString *lastName = @"Campbell";
```

Here is another NSString constructor, stringWithFormat:, that is used often when other variables and objects are used to compose a new string:

```
NSString *n = [NSString stringWithFormat:@"%@ %@", firstName, lastName];
```

This constructor, stringWithContentsOfFile:encoding:error:, is used to create a new NSString object based on the contents of a file.

```
NSString *fileName = @"/Users/Shared/report.txt";
NSString *fileContents = [NSString
            stringWithContentsOfFile:fileName
                        encoding:NSStringEncodingConversionAllowLossy
                            error:nil];
```

# NSMutableString

Sometimes you want to be able to add or remove characters to a string as your program executes. For instance, you may want to maintain a log of changes users make in your program and you don't want to create new strings each time a change is made. These situations call for NSSMutableString.

You can use the same constructors to create NSMutableString objects except for the shortcut where you assign an object to a string contained in @"". To create a simple NSMutableString, use the stringWithString: constructor.

```
NSMutableString *alpha = [NSMutableString stringWithString:@"A"];
```

## Inserting Strings

You can insert strings into a mutable string at any point in the list of characters that make up the mutable string. You just have to be sure that the insertion point that you specify is in range of the list of characters. Don't attempt to insert a string in position 20 if your string is only 10 characters long. You can find out the length of a string by sending the length message to the string.

To insert a string, you will need to specify both the string that you want to insert and the starting position. Here is how you would insert a B into the alpha mutable string:

```
[alpha insertString:@"B"
          atIndex:[alpha length]];
```

Here you are sending the insertString:atIndex: message. The first parameter is @"B", which is the string you want to add to the mutable string A. The atIndex: parameter is the length of the alpha string since you want to append the B to the end of the A string to produce @"AB".

If you really just want to append a string, there is an even easier method available to do that. You can send the appendString: message, which only requires the string parameter. The insertion point is not required because it is assumed that the string will be appended to the end of the mutable string.

```
[alpha appendString:@"C"];
```

## Deleting Strings

Just as you can add strings to a mutable string, you can remove parts of a mutable string. When you are deleting strings, you will need to specify both a starting point and a length. There is a composite type called NSRange that can help with that. NSRange has two variables associated with it, location and length. You need to create one of these composite types first before sending the deleteCharactorsInRange: message to the mutable string.

```
NSRange range;
range.location = 1;
range.length = 1;
[alpha deleteCharactersInRange:range];
```

This code will delete the B from the ABC string you created in the previous steps.

---

▓ **Note** When you use NSRange, you should keep in mind that strings are stored as a list of letters that start with the index of 0.

---

# Find and Replace

Anyone who has used a word processor knows how convenient the find and replace function can be. You just supply the program with the text that you want to replace and the text that you want in its place. NSMutableString also has this ability.

To do find and replace with a mutable string you will need to define a range and supply the string that you are looking for and the string that you put in the first string's place. There are also search options that you can specify.

```
range.location = 0;
range.length = 2;

[alpha replaceOccurrencesOfString:@"AC"
                       withString:@"ABCDEFGHI"
                          options:NSLiteralSearch
                            range:range];
```

The first thing you are doing here is reusing the NSRange range variable to specify what part of the string you want to look at. You are going to start at the beginning and search the entire length of the string.

Next, you define the string that you want to replace, @"AC", and the string that you want to use as a replacement, @"ABCDEFGHI".

In the options you set the NSLiteralSearch option. This means that the method will require an exact match for your strings. You could also specify NSCaseInsensitiveSearch to ignore case and NSRegularExpressionSearch, which lets you use a regular expression.

---

▓ **Note** Regular expressions are a tool used to search strings for patterns. They are used in many programming languages. A full explanation of regular expressions is out of the scope of this book, but worth looking into if you spend a lot of time working with strings.

---

The last parameter is the range variable that you set up before the message.

# CHAPTER 7

# Numbers

## NSNumber

NSNumber is the class used in Objective-C to work with numbers. NSNumber gives you a way to turn floating point and integer values into object-oriented number objects. While you can't use NSNumber objects in expressions, NSNumber objects become useful when complicated formatting is required.

NSNumber objects can be created with many different constructors, but the most common way you'll see NSNumber objects created is with the @ symbol followed by a number.

```
NSNumber *num1 = @1;
NSNumber *num2 = @2.25;
```

Sometimes you may want to use special constructors that are matched to numbers stored in a particular way.

```
NSNumber *num3 = [NSNumber numberWithInteger:3];
NSNumber *num4 = [NSNumber numberWithFloat:4.44];
```

## Converting to Primitive Data Types

NSNumber objects can't be used in expressions, but NSNumber has some built-in functions that will return the object in a primitive data type form. You will have to use these functions to convert numbers before using them in expressions.

```
CGFloat result = [num1 floatValue] + [num2 floatValue];
```

The function used above is floatValue but there are more like intValue and doubleValue that match primitive data types from C programming like int and double. stringValue is another function that will return the number formatted as a string, which can be useful in reports.

# Formatting Numbers

NSNumber becomes very useful when you want to format numbers for displays in reports and presentations. When used with the NSNumberFormatter class you can output numbers as localized currency, scientific notation, and they can even be spelled out.

To do this, you must create a new number formatter and then set the formatting style that you want to use.

```
NSNumberFormatter *formatter = [[NSNumberFormatter alloc] init];
formatter.numberStyle = NSNumberFormatterCurrencyStyle;
```

Then you can send the stringFromNumber: message to get the formatted number. Here is an example of doing this in the context of using NSLog to write a message to the console:

```
NSLog(@"Formatted num2 = %@", [formatter stringFromNumber:num2]);
```

This will output **$2.25** from my computer since I'm set up in the United States. Your output will differ depending on the locale that you have set on your Mac or iOS device.

# Converting Strings into Numbers

You can also convert a string into a number. If you have a number represented as a string, you can use a number formatter to convert the string into an NSNumber object.

Just change the number formatter style to the style in which the number was stored. Then create a new NSNumber object with the NSNumberFormatter numberFromString: message. Here is how to convert the string "**two point two five**" into the number **2.25**:

```
formatter.numberStyle = NSNumberFormatterSpellOutStyle;
NSNumber *num5 = [formatter numberFromString:@"two point two five"];
```

# CHAPTER 8

# Arrays

## NSArray

NSArray is a class used to organize objects in lists. NSArray can maintain an index of objects, search for objects, and enumerate through the list. Enumeration is the process of moving through a list one item at a time and performing an action on each item in the list.

To create an array, you include a comma-separate list of objects enclosed in square brackets and started with the @ symbol.

```
NSArray *numbers = @[@-2, @-1, @0, @1, @2];
NSArray *letters = @[@"A", @"B", @"C", @"D", @"E", @"F"];
```

The NSArray object numbers has a list of NSNumber objects, while letters has a list of strings. Any object can be put into an NSArray object, but not primitives like NSInteger.

### Referencing Objects

You put objects in arrays so that you have an easy way of getting references to these objects later. The general way of getting these references is to send an objectAtIndex: message to the array. Here is how to get the number object reference from the second position in the numbers array:

```
NSNumber *num = [numbers objectAtIndex:1];
```

If you know that you want the last object in the list, you use lastObject to return the last object in the list.

---

**Note**  Array indexes in Objective-C start with 0.

---

```
NSNumber *lastNum = [numbers lastObject];
```

Sometimes you might already have a reference to the object in question, but you want to find out the index number that corresponds to the object's position in the array. You can use indexOfObject: to get this information.

```
NSUInteger index = [numbers indexOfObject:num];
```

## Enumeration

Enumeration is the process of moving through a list one item at time. Usually, you will be performing some type of action on each item, like writing out the object's contents to the log or modifying a property on the object.

Blocks, or anonymous functions, are used to perform enumeration with arrays. Blocks are functions that are not attached to an object. You can define a block on enclosing lines of code in curly brackets. Blocks can be treated like objects, which means that you can pass a block to an enumeration method just like you could do for a variable or an object.

---

⁑ **Note**   Blocks deserve their own treatment, apart from their use in arrays, and so more details about using blocks will be covered in Chapter 20.

---

Let's say you want to go through the array of numbers and print out each number's value when squared. You could enumerate through the list using the NSArray enumerateObjectsUsingBlock: method. This method will give you a reference to the current object, which you can use to perform this simple operation.

```
[numbers enumerateObjectsUsingBlock:^(id obj, NSUInteger idx, BOOL *stop) {
    NSLog(@"obj ^ 2= %f", [obj floatValue] * [obj floatValue]);
}];
```

All of the code after the colon is the block code. This block starts with the ^ symbol. Then you can see a comma-separated list of parameters followed up by curly brackets. The code inside the curly brackets is the block, and the parameters declared in the parentheses are the variables that the block can reference.

# NSMutableArray

More often than not, you need to be able to add and remove items from an array as your program executes code. You could be maintaining a list of action items or video game characters. When you need to do this, you can use NSMutableArray.

NSMutableArray does everything that NSArray does except that it gives you the ability to change the contents of the array. You can add and remove items and do other types of manipulations on objects in mutable arrays.

You can't use the shortcut for array creation here, though, and `NSMutableArray` will require you to use a constructor, like this:

```
NSMutableArray *mArray = [NSMutableArray arrayWithArray:@[@-2, @-1, @0]];
```

The constructor used above is arrayWithArray: and you just passed on an NSArray object to this constructor to get started.

To add an object to a mutable array, you use the `addObject:` message.

```
[mArray addObject:@1];
```

To remove an object, you must use the `removeObject:` message and pass a reference to the object that you want to remove.

```
[mArray removeObject:@1];
```

If you want to exchange one object with another, you can use the method `exchangeObjectAtIndex:withObjectAtIndex:`.

```
[mArray exchangeObjectAtIndex:0 withObjectAtIndex:1];
```

This will take whatever is in position 0 and switch with whatever is in position 1.

There are many other variations of these functions available to you. You can remove all items, add arrays of items into the mutable array, or insert items or arrays of items at a specific starting point in the array.

# CHAPTER 9

# Dictionaries

## NSDictionary

NSDictionary is a class used to organize objects in lists using keys and values. NSDictionary can maintain an index of objects and let you retrieve an object if you have the right key. Usually, the key will be an NSString object while the value will be whatever type of object you are indexing.

To create a dictionary, you include a comma-separate list of key value pairs enclosed in curly brackets and started with the @ symbol.

```
NSDictionary *d1 = @{@"one": @1, @"two": @2, @"three": @3};
```

This creates a dictionary of NSNumber objects that you can reference with their string keys. So, the key string @"one" can be used to retrieve the NSNumber object 1.

### Referencing Objects

You put objects in dictionaries so that you have an efficient way of getting references to these objects bases on keys. The general way of getting these references is to send an objectForKey: message to the dictionary. Here is how to get the number referenced by the key @"one":

```
NSNumber *n1 =[d1 objectForKey:@"one"];
```

### Enumeration

Enumeration is the process of moving through a list one item at time. Usually, you will be performing some type of action on each item, like writing out the object's contents to the log or modifying a property on the object.

You can enumerate through a dictionary in almost the same way as you do with an array. But you will get a reference to each key in the dictionary as well as each object.

```
[d1 enumerateKeysAndObjectsUsingBlock:^(id key, id obj, BOOL *stop) {
    NSLog(@"key = %@, value = %@", key, obj);
}];
```

Just like with the array enumeration procedure discussed in Chapter 8, the block code declaration starts with the ^ character and the block code is enclosed in the curly brackets, { }.

Here is the output that would be generated with this message:

```
key = one, value = 1
key = two, value = 2
key = three, value = 3
```

# NSMutableDictionary

NSDictionary is an immutable object, so once you create an NSDictionary object you can't add or remove items from the dictionary. If you need to add or remove items from a dictionary, you must use the NSMutableDictionary class.

You can't use the shortcut for array creation here, though, and NSMutableDictionary requires you to use a constructor, like this:

```
NSMutableDictionary *md1 = [[NSMutableDictionary alloc] init];
```

The easiest thing to do is to follow the alloc and init pattern to create an empty dictionary to which you can add objects. When you are ready to add an object to the dictionary, you will need a key and the value that you want to add. These two parameters will be supplied to the setObject: for Key: method.

```
[md1 setObject:@4 forKey:@"four"];
```

To remove an object, send the removeObjectForKey: message and supply the key.

```
[md1 removeObjectForKey:@"four"];
```

You can remove every object from a mutable dictionary by sending the removeAllObjects message.

```
[md1 removeAllObjects];
```

# For Loops

## For Loops Defined

Loops are used when you want to repeat a similar type of task many times. For loops are used when you know beforehand how many times you want to repeat a similar line of code. Here is a for loop that will write to the console window 10 times:

```
for (int i=0; i<10; i++) {
    NSLog(@"i = %i", i);
}
```

This for loop will produce this output:

```
i = 0
i = 1
i = 2
i = 3
i = 4
i = 5
i = 6
i = 7
i = 8
i = 9
```

Let's take a closer loop at the parts of this loop. The first thing is the for keyword. This lets the compiler know that you are coding a for loop.

Next, you have a series of code lines enclosed in parenthesis: (int i=0; i<10; i++). These lines of code specify a starting condition (int i=0;), an ending condition (i<10), and an increment instruction (i++). This means that the loop will repeat 10 times by starting at 0 while the variable i increases by 1 each time the loop executes as long as i is less than 10.

Finally, you have a code block defined by curly brackets, { }. The code contained in these curly brackets will execute each time you go through the loop. In the example above, the code block had only one line of code, NSLog(@"i = %i", i);. Notice that the variable i, sometimes called the counter variable, is in scope and you can use i in the code block.

# For Loops and Arrays

More often than not, you will use a for loop to go through a list and do something with each object in that list. Let's assume that you have an array named list that has a five NSNumber objects ranging from -2.0 to 2.0.

```
NSArray *list = @[@-2.0, @-1.0, @0.0, @1.0, @2.0];
```

Let's say that you want to construct a string that includes all values in list but spelled out with words. For example, you want a string minus two, minus one, etc. You would need to use NSNumberFormatter and an NSMutableString, both of which have been covered in the chapters on numbers and strings.

Just to set this up, let's get the number formatter, mutable string, and array before you go into the for loop.

```
NSArray *list = @[@-2.0, @-1.0, @0.0, @1.0, @2.0];
NSMutableString *report = [[NSMutableString alloc] init];
NSNumberFormatter *formatter = [[NSNumberFormatter alloc] init];
formatter.numberStyle = NSNumberFormatterSpellOutStyle;
```

Note that you are specifying NSNumberFormatterSpellOutStyle here so that the number formatter can give you the value of each number object spelled out.

Since you want the for loop to move through each number in the array list, you will need to find out how many objects are contained in list. NSArray objects have a count property that you can use to get the number of objects contained in the array, and you can use this value directly in the for loop.

```
for (int i=0; i<list.count; i++) {
    NSNumber *num = [list objectAtIndex:i];
    NSString *spelledOutNum = [formatter stringFromNumber:num];
    [report appendString:spelledOutNum];
    [report appendString:@", "];
}
```

What you are doing above is going through each object in list and getting a reference to the number in the list that corresponds to the index that is associated with the current value of i.

Next, you use the number formatter to get the spelled-out string version of the number. Finally, you append this spelled-out string value to the end of the mutable string. Here is what the output would look like:

```
report = minus two, minus one, zero, one, two,
```

# CHAPTER 11

# While Loops

## While Loops Defined

Like for loops, while loops are used when you want to repeat a similar type of task many times. While loops are used when you want to execute a line of code many times until a condition is met. Here is a while loop that will write to the console window 10 times:

```
int i = 0;

while (i < 10) {
    NSLog(@"i = %i", i);
    i++;
}
```

This while loop will produce this output:

```
i = 0
i = 1
i = 2
i = 3
i = 4
i = 5
i = 6
i = 7
i = 8
i = 9
```

The loop above does the same thing as the for loop from Chapter 10, but note that the specifications for the loop are in different spots. The first thing that you will notice is that you need to have a counter variable on hand to use in a while loop. You can't just put the counter variable right in the body of the loop like you did before. So you need a separate line of code before the while loop to declare and assign the counter variable.

```
int i = 0;
```

Then you have the while loop itself that is started with the while keyword. In the parentheses after the while keyword is the ending condition, (i < 10). This means that the loop will go on as long as the value of i is less than 10.

Finally, you have a code block defined by curly brackets. The code contained in these curly brackets will execute each time you go through the loop. You have one line of code, NSLog(@"i = %i", i);, to write to the log. You also increment the counter variable in this code block, i++;.

---

▨ **Note**    It's important to remember to increment the counter variable here. If you don't do this, then i will never go beyond 10. The loop will never end, which will effectively cause your program to hang until a user terminates it.

---

## While Loops and Arrays

Now let's go ahead and repeat the example from Chapter 10 where you formatted a list of numbers in an array with a loop. This is the array and other objects that you worked with in Chapter 10:

```
NSArray *list = @[@-2.0, @-1.0, @0.0, @1.0, @2.0];
NSMutableString *report = [[NSMutableString alloc] init];
NSNumberFormatter *formatter = [[NSNumberFormatter alloc] init];
formatter.numberStyle = NSNumberFormatterSpellOutStyle;
```

You are going to do the same thing you did in Chapter 10, but you will use the while loop instead.

```
int i = 0;

while(i < list.count) {
    NSNumber *num = [list objectAtIndex:i];
    NSString *spelledOutNum = [formatter stringFromNumber:num];
    [report appendString:spelledOutNum];
    [report appendString:@", "];
    i++;
}
```

What you are doing above is going through each object in the list and getting a reference to the number in the list that corresponds to the index that is associated with the current value of i.

Next, you use the number formatter to get the spelled-out string version of the number. Finally, you append this spelled-out string value to the end of the mutable string. Here is what the value of report would look like:

```
report = minus two, minus one, zero, one, two,
```

# CHAPTER 12

# Do While Loops

## Do While Loops Defined

Do while loops are used for the same reasons as for loops and while loops. The syntax is different, and do while loops are notable because the code in the block will execute at least once. This is because the ending condition is not evaluated until the end of the loop. Here is how you would code a do while loop to count to 10:

```
int i = 0;

do{
    NSLog(@"i = %i", i);
    i++;
}while (i <10);
```

This do while loop will produce this output:

```
i = 0
i = 1
i = 2
i = 3
i = 4
i = 5
i = 6
i = 7
i = 8
i = 9
```

The loop above does the same thing as the for loop from Chapter 10 and the while loop in Chapter 11. The specifications for the do while loop are similar to the while loop but they are located in different lines of code.

Like the while loop, you need to have a counter variable on hand.

```
int i = 0;
```

Then you have the do while loop itself that is started with the do keyword. Immediately after the do keyword you have a code block defined by curly brackets. The code contained in these curly brackets will execute each time you go through the loop. You have one line of code, NSLog(@"i = %i", i);, to write to the log. You also increment the counter variable in this code block, i++;.

The condition (i < 10) is after the while keyword right after the code block. This means that the loop will go on as long as the value of i is less than 10.

---

▓ **Note**    It's important to remember to increment the counter variable here. If you don't do this, then i will never go beyond 10, and the loop will never end, which will effectively cause your program to hang until a user terminates it.

---

## Do While Loops and Arrays

Now let's go ahead and repeat the example from Chapter 10 and Chapter 11 where you formatted a list of numbers in an array with a loop. This is the array and other objects that you worked with in Chapter 10 and Chapter 11:

```
NSArray *list = @[@-2.0, @-1.0, @0.0, @1.0, @2.0];
NSMutableString *report = [[NSMutableString alloc] init];
NSNumberFormatter *formatter = [[NSNumberFormatter alloc] init];
formatter.numberStyle = NSNumberFormatterSpellOutStyle;
```

You are going to use the do while loop instead.

```
int i = 0;

do {
    NSNumber *num = [list objectAtIndex:i];
    NSString *spelledOutNum = [formatter stringFromNumber:num];
    [report appendString:spelledOutNum];
    [report appendString:@", "];
    i++;
}while(i < list.count);

NSLog(@"report = %@", report);
```

You will end up with a mutablable string that you can write out to the console log. The output will look like this:

```
report = minus two, minus one, zero, one, two,
```

# CHAPTER 13

# For-Each Loops

## For-Each Loops Defined

For-each loops are a more specific type of loop that can only be used with collection objects like NSArray and NSDictionary. You can use a for loop when you want to move through a list of objects to perform an action on each object in the list.

For example, let's take the array example from Chapter 8.

```
NSArray *numbers = @[@-2, @-1, @0, @1, @2];
```

In Chapter 8, you used the enumeration method with a block to go through the list and square each number. You can use a for loop as an alternative to the enumeration method.

```
for (NSNumber *num in numbers){
    NSLog(@"num ^ 2= %f", [num floatValue] * [num floatValue]);
}
```

This loop starts with the for keyword before a specification in parentheses. The specification starts with an object type (NSNumber) and a variable that will give you a reference to the current object in the list, (*num).

Next, you can see the keyword in followed by the array (numbers). Taken all together, you can read this as "for each number num in the array numbers, do something." The something here is defined in the code block that comes right after the first part of the loop. It will go through the entire array and square each number, producing the following output:

```
num ^ 2= 4.000000
num ^ 2= 1.000000
num ^ 2= 0.000000
num ^ 2= 1.000000
num ^ 2= 4.000000
```

# For Loops with NSDictionary

Dictionaries are a little bit more complicated than arrays because dictionaries maintain a list of keys and objects. You might expect that a for each loop used on a dictionary would yield a list of objects; however it turns out that you will just get a list of the dictionary keys.

So, if you code a for each loop with an NSDictionary, as in

```
NSDictionary *d1 = @{@"one": @1, @"two": @2, @"three": @3};
for (id object in d1){
    NSLog(@"object = %@", object);
}
```

you will get output that lists out all the keys like this :

```
object = one
object = two
object = three
```

If you want to output values in the dictionary, you will need to send the objectForKey: message to the dictionary.

```
for (id object in d1){
    NSNumber *num = [d1 objectForKey:object];
    NSLog(@"num = %@", num);
}
```

This for loop will print out the values of the objects.

```
num = 1
num = 2
num = 3
```

# CHAPTER 14

# If Statements

## If Statements Defined

If statements are used when you want to make a choice to execute code based on the trueness of a condition. To make this work, you evaluate an expression that uses relational operators to yield a YES or NO result. If you evaluate an express to be true, then you can execute the code; otherwise you can ignore the code.

You need the if keyword and an expression here along with a code block to use the if statement.

```
if(1 < 2){
    NSLog(@"That is true");
}
```

The statement is saying that if 1 is less than 2, then execute the code that will print out the string "That is true" to the console log.

## Else Keyword

You can also define an alternate action with the else keyword. This gives you a way of executing either one of two actions based on the results of the expression that you are evaluating.

```
if(1 < 2){
    NSLog(@"That is true");
}
else{
    NSLog(@"Not true");
}
```

## Nested If Else

Each if statement can contain nested if statements. This gives you a way of testing multiple conditions. Generally speaking, it's best to limit yourself to three nested if statements at most. Here is what a nested if statement looks like:

```
if(1 > 2){
    NSLog(@"True");
}
else{
    if(3 > 4){
        NSLog(@"True");
    }
    else{
        NSLog(@"Not True");
    }
}
```

## If Statements and Variables

Generally you will see if statements used along with variables that are used to keep track of the state of a program. You can use variables inside the parentheses as part of the expression in the if statement or you can test the variables directly.

```
BOOL isTrue = 1 == 2;

if(isTrue){
    NSLog(@"isTrue = %@", isTrue ? @"YES" : @"NO");
    NSLog(@"That was a true statement.");
}
else{
    NSLog(@"isTrue = %@", isTrue ? @"YES" : @"NO");
    NSLog(@"That was not a true statement.");
}
```

In the code above, you are assigning the result of an expression to the Boolean variable isTrue and then testing this later on with an if statement.

Here is what you will see in the console log if you test this code for yourself:

```
isTrue = NO
That was not a true statement.
```

## CHAPTER 15

# Switch Statements

## Switch Statements Defined

Switch statements are used to execute code based on the value of an integer. To make a switch statement work, you need to define a level variable and then you need to write a code block for each possible value of the level variable that you expect.

For this chapter, let's assume you are writing code to help you do some geometry work. You have different shapes that you need to work with and you want to calculate the area of each shape. You can keep track of what type of shape you are working with by using an NSInteger variable like shape.

```
NSInteger shape = 0;
```

Each value of the NSInteger shape will correspond to a type of shape. Zero could be a square, one could be a parallelogram, and two could be a circle. Variables like shape are called a level variable because they represent possible levels.

For the purposes of this example, you also need a variable to store the results of any calculation you make, which is why you have a float variable named area.

```
float area;
```

### Switch Keyword

Now, let's get to the switch statement itself. To start a switch statement, you need the switch keyword followed by the level variable in parentheses. Also, you should use curly brackets to create a code block for the switch statement.

```
switch (shape) {

}
```

### Case Keyword

Next, you can define code blocks that will be associated with each value that the level variable can take on. You use the case keyword to associate each possible value with a code block.

```
switch (shape) {

    case 0:{
        float length = 3;
        area = length * length;
        NSLog(@"Square area is %f", area);
        break;
    }

}
```

What you see above is the `case` keyword followed by the value that you are testing for, which is 0. Then you have a colon followed by curly brackets that define the code block that will execute whenever the value of shape is 0.

## break Keyword

At the end of the code block above you can see the break keyword. This keyword will return control the program back to the main program and outside of the case statement. If this statement didn't appear, then every line of code after would execute whenever the first case was true (switch statements stop evaluating the level variable once it finds a true value).

## Complete Switch Statement

Here is what the statement looks like with multiple case statements:

```
switch (shape) {

    case 0:{
        float length = 3;
        area = length * length;
        NSLog(@"Square area is %f", area);
        break;
    }
    case 1:{
        float base = 16;
        float height = 24;
        area = base * height;
        NSLog(@"Parallelogram area is %f", area);
        break;
    } default:{
        area = -999;
        NSLog(@"No Shape Specified");
        break;
    }

}
```

# Default Case

If you look closely at the code above, you can see that there is a `default` keyword. This keyword is used to define a default case, which is a way to define a code block that will execute if none of the other conditions are met. So, if the value of shape happened to be 6 and had no code block defined, you would be sure that at least the code that was included in the default case would execute.

Here is what you will find in the console log if you run the code from this chapter:

```
Square area is 9.000000
```

# CHAPTER 16

# Defining Classes

## Classes

I covered objects when I demonstrated the Objective-C objects used to work with strings, number, arrays, and dictionaries. Objects are an essential object-oriented programming pattern. While you will often simply use Foundation objects that are already set up for you, usually you will need to define your own types of objects customized for your app.

You can use classes to define your own object types. Classes are code definitions that are used to create objects. The primary purpose of coding class definitions is to express an entity that has attributes and behaviors.

Attributes are called properties when coding classes and behaviors are called methods. Properties are used to describe an object while methods are used to get objects to perform an action.

You need to do two important tasks when defining a class: code an interface and code an implementation.

## Class Interfaces

You use a class interface to specify the name of the class and the properties and methods that make up the class. Here is how you would set up a class called `Project`:

```
#import <Foundation/Foundation.h>

@interface Project : NSObject

@end
```

The line of the code that begins with the `#import` imports the Foundation framework. This framework is needed whenever you want to work with Objective-C classes like `NSObject` or `NSString` (which you almost always do).

In particular, you need to reference `NSObject` since that will be your base class. A base class is what your class will be derived from and provides a starting point for you. `NSObject` provides the object creation methods you need to make your objects work like objects (such as `alloc` and `init`).

In the line that starts with @interface keyword, you can use the name of the class, Project, and the base class NSObject, which comes after the colon.

The @interface keyword must be matched with the @end keyword.

# Property Forward Declarations

Properties require a forward declaration that is coded in the class interface. These belong in the space between the @interface line and @end line.

```
#import <Foundation/Foundation.h>

@interface Project : NSObject
```

**@property(strong) NSString *name;**

```
@end
```

Property forward declarations start with the @property keyword followed by a property descriptor in parenthesis. See Table 16-1 for a list of the possible parameter descriptors that you can use.

*Table 16-1.*  *Parameter Descriptors*

| Attribute | Description |
| --- | --- |
| Readwrite | The property needs both a getter and a setter (default). |
| Readonly | The property only needs a getter (objects cannot set this property). |
| strong | The property will have a strong relationship. |
| weak | The property will be set to nil when the destination object is deallocated. |
| assign | The property will simply use assignment (used with primitive types). |
| Copy | The property returns a copy and must implement the NSCopying protocol. |
| retain | A retain message will be sent in the setter method. |
| nonatomic | Specifies the property is not atomic (not locked while being accessed). |

The next two parts of the property forward declaration are the datatype and the name of the property. You can read this forward declaration as defining a property name of type NSString that Project will have a strong relationship with.

⬛ **Note** Terms like strong, retain, and weak have to do with how memory management is handled for the property value. Both strong and retain mean that your class objects will always retain a reference to the property value, which guarantees that the object will stay in scope for as long as you need it. Property descriptors weak and assign don't provide this guarantee.

# Method Forward Declarations

Methods also need forward declarations. While properties describe an object, methods represent actions that an object can take. Here is how you would add a forward declaration to the Project class:

```
#import <Foundation/Foundation.h>

@interface Project : NSObject

@property(strong) NSString *name;

-(void)generateReport;

@end
```

Method forward declarations start with the minus sign followed by the return type in parenthesis. This method has a void return type, but you can have any datatype or class as a return type for a method.

After that is the method's signature, which I will talk more about once you see a method that includes parameters. Here is an example of a method that includes parameters:

```
#import <Foundation/Foundation.h>

@interface Project : NSObject

@property(strong) NSString *name;

-(void)generateReport;
-(void)generateReportAndAddThisString:(NSString *)string
                   andThenAddThisDate:(NSDate *)date;

@end
```

In this parameter, you can see that the method signature is broken up into two parts. Each part has a parameter and a parameter descriptor separated by a colon. In Objective-C, method signatures are a collection of parameter descriptors and parameters. When you have no parameters (like the first method), you just have a parameter descriptor to describe the method.

# Implementing Classes

Defining the class interface is the first part of the process of defining a class. The next part is called the implementation because this is where you provide the code implementation that makes the class objects work.

To start implementing a class, you use the @implementation keyword along with the class name.

```
#import "Project.h"

@implementation Project

@end
```

The first line of code is importing the Project forward declarations into this file so the class is aware of what needs to be implemented.

---

▨ **Note**  While it is not required, usually class interfaces and implementations will be coded in separate files. Interface files end with the .h file extension and are sometimes called header files. Implementation files end with the .m file extension and are sometimes called code files.

---

The implementation begins with the @implementation keyword followed by the name of the class Project. Implementations end with the @end keyword. Now, you need to implement the properties and methods.

Properties are implemented for you automatically and you don't need to take any action to make properties work.

## Implementing Methods

When you implement a method, you repeat the forward declaration of the method from the interface. But you add a code block and the code that you need to get the method to do something.

```
#import "Project.h"

@implementation Project

-(void)generateReport{
    NSLog(@"This is a report!");
}

@end
```

When you implement a method that includes parameters, you can reference those parameter values in your code.

```
#import "Project.h"

@implementation Project

-(void)generateReport{
    NSLog(@"This is a report!");
}

-(void)generateReportAndAddThisString:(NSString *)string
                        andThenAddThisDate:(NSDate *)date{
    [self generateReport];
    NSLog(@"%@", string);
    NSLog(@"Date: %@", date);
}

@end
```

## Private Properties and Methods

The procedures above define properties and methods publically. This means that other objects can reference these properties and use those methods. Classes that are derived from this class can use and override these properties and methods. If you want to prevent that from happening to make properties and methods private, you can use a class extension.

## Class Extensions

Class extensions give you a way to extend a class interface in the implementation file. Since other classes will be importing the interface file that ends with the .h extension (the header file), they will not be able to access anything with forward declarations that are defined in a class extension.

You can put a class extension in the implementation file like this:

```
#import "Project.h"

@interface Project()

@property(strong) NSArray *listOfTasks;

-(void)generateAnotherReport;

@end

@implementation Project

-(void)generateReport{
    NSLog(@"This is a report!");
}

-(void)generateReportAndAddThisString:(NSString *)string
                 andThenAddThisDate:(NSDate *)date{
    [self generateReport];
    NSLog(@"%@", string);
    NSLog(@"Date: %@", date);
}

-(void)generateAnotherReport{
    NSLog(@"Another report!");
}

@end
```

The class extension looks like the interface but has empty parenthesis after the class name. The forward declarations that are in the class extension above follow the same rules as the other forward declarations for properties and methods. Class extensions must end with the @end keyword (each @interface requires a matching @end).

## Local Instance Variables

Sometimes you need storage variables that don't merit a property declaration. For instance, sometimes you want to have a "counter" or "progress" variable or a variable that maintains a log. These are needed but don't really describe the object so they don't merit the same treatment as a property.

Instead, you can use an instance variable or ivar in these situations. Instance variables can be included right in the class extension, like this:

```
#import "Project.h"

@interface Project() {
    int counter;
    NSString *log;
}

@property(strong) NSArray *listOfTasks;

-(void)generateAnotherReport;

@end

@implementation Project

-(void)generateReport{
    NSLog(@"This is a report!");
}

-(void)generateReportAndAddThisString:(NSString *)string
                   andThenAddThisDate:(NSDate *)date{
    [self generateReport];
    NSLog(@"%@", string);
    NSLog(@"Date: %@", date);
}

-(void)generateAnotherReport{
    NSLog(@"Another report!");
}

@end
```

# CHAPTER 17

# Class Methods

## Class Methods Defined

In Chapter 16, we described how to define classes with properties and methods. The type of method we focused on was instance methods. Instance methods are methods can only be used with objects. When you want to use an instance method, you send a message to an object.

For instance, if you want to send the generateReport message to a Project object, you first need create the object and then send the message right to the object.

```
Project *p = [[Project alloc] init];
[p generateReport];
```

Class methods are like instance methods except that they can only be used with classes. When you want to use a class method, you must send the message to the class. If you look closely at the constructor above, you can see that you are already using a class method called alloc.

## Coding Class Methods

If you want to create your own class method, you need to start in the class interface. Let's code a forward declaration for a class method that prints out a time stamp called printTimeStamp. You can add this to the class that you started in the last chapter.

```
#import <Foundation/Foundation.h>

@interface Project : NSObject

@property(strong) NSString *name;

-(void)generateReport;
-(void)generateReportAndAddThisString:(NSString *)string
                 andThenAddThisDate:(NSDate *)date;
+(void)printTimeStamp;

@end
```

This method looks like the instance methods that you already coded, except that it has a plus sign (+) in front of the return type.

The next step is to implement this method, which you must do in the implementation for Project. Note that some of the code from Chapter 16 is omitted here to avoid making this example too long and distracting.

```
#import "Project.h"

@implementation Project

+(void)printTimeStamp{
    NSLog(@"Timestamp: %@", [NSDate date]);
}

@end
```

You need to use the plus sign here again to define this as a class method, but the coding follows the same pattern as the instance methods.

When you want to use the printTimeStamp method, you send the message directly to the class. You don't need to create an object first here.

```
[Project printTimeStamp];
```

This message will print the following out to the console log:

```
Timestamp: 2014-10-30 18:13:01 +0000
```

# CHAPTER 18

# Inheritance

When you want to code a new class that shares most of the properties and methods of another class, you can use inheritance. A class that is inherited from another class takes on all the properties and methods of the superclass.

You use inheritance when you want to leverage the work that has already been completed and then add more properties and methods to customize the new class. This pattern gives us code reuse.

You saw examples of inheritance in Chapter 16: when you created the Project class, you inherited NSObject. This gave Project all the methods and properties of NSObject.

A more interesting application happens when you use this technique with your object graph. For instance, let's assume that now you want to create a new class that's like Project but has a few key differences.

## Creating Subclasses

To create a new subclass, you can follow the same pattern that was laid out in Chapter 16. You define an interface and implementation. The difference here is that you will choose Project instead of NSObject as the superclass.

```
#import "Project.h"

@interface SpecialProject : Project

@end
```

The two things to note in the interface above are that you are importing **Project.h** (and not Foundation as before) and you now have Project after the colon and not NSObject, indicating that Project is the superclass and that SpecialProject is your subclass.

The implementation for SpecialProject is straightforward and resembles what you did for the original Project class.

```
#import "SpecialProject.h"

@implementation SpecialProject

@end
```

If you were to use SpecialProject right now, it would behave just like Project. Now you can add additional properties and methods to customize SpecialProject. This is called extending a class.

# Extending Classes

To extend a class, you can add properties and methods to the subclass. Your subclass is SpecialProject. Let's add a method named generateSpecialReport to your SpecialProject class.

```
#import "Project.h"

@interface SpecialProject : Project

-(void)generateSpecialReport;

@end
```

Now, of course, you need to implement this method.

```
#import "SpecialProject.h"

@implementation SpecialProject

-(void)generateSpecialReport{
    NSLog(@"This is a special report!");
}

@end
```

The procedure to extend classes is identical to adding properties and methods as you normally do. What makes this a good tool is that you can share the code for the methods that are common among a type of class.

# Overriding Methods

Another thing you can do is override a method from your superclass. Overriding a method means that you are going to write your own version of a method with the exact same signature (the collection of parameter descriptors). The code in your method will be different so this means that objects from the inherited class will behave differently even though they get the same message sent to them as the superclass.

Let's say you want to make sure that SpecialProject objects always print out the special report even if the generateReport message from the Project superclass is sent.

What you need to do first is code generateReport method in the `SpecialProject` interface.

```
#import "Project.h"

@interface SpecialProject : Project

-(void)generateSpecialReport;
-(void)generateReport;

@end
```

Then you need to code a new implementation of generateReport and have that method send a message to generateSpecialReport. Often in this situation, you will also send a message to the super's implementation of the method, which you can do by sending a message to super.

```
#import "SpecialProject.h"

@implementation SpecialProject

-(void)generateSpecialReport{
    NSLog(@"This is a special report!");
}

-(void)generateReport{
    [super generateReport];
    [self generateSpecialReport];
}

@end
```

# Instance Variable Visibility

When I discussed instance variables, or ivars, in Chapter 16, the use case for these was straightforward. If your class needed data storage that didn't really describe an attribute of the object (and therefore shouldn't have a property), then you would just use an ivar.

Since you added ivars to the class extension, the class that you were implementing in that file could only use them. These ivars are considered private because they are only visible to the class that they are coded in.

## Visibility Levels

When you are planning on using inheritance with your object graph, you may want instance variables to have different levels of visibility. The term "visibility" refers to the other entities' access to the variable. Instance variables can either be private, protected, or public. When you want to have different visibility levels, you must code your instance variables in the interface, which should be located in a header file since this is the file that other classes will be importing.

## Private Instance Variables

Private instance variables can only be used in the class they are coded in. To make an instance variable private, you would declare the instance variable in the class interface. Let's say you wanted to add some NSString objects to act as logs for all of your Project classes. To add a private log to be used in Project objects, you would do something like this in the Project interface:

```
#import <Foundation/Foundation.h>

@interface Project : NSObject {
    @private NSString *log1;
}

@property(strong) NSString *name;

-(void)generateReport;
-(void)generateReportAndAddThisString:(NSString *)string
                andThenAddThisDate:(NSDate *)date;
+(void)printTimeStamp;

@end
```

You must use the @private keyword to designate that log1 will have private visibility. This means you can use log1 in your Project methods, but not in your SpecialProject methods.

## Protected Instance Methods

Instance variables with protected visibility can be accessed by methods in the class they are coded in as well as any derived classes. So, if you wanted to have an NSString log variable that can be used by Project and SpecialProject, you would need to make it protected by using the @protected keyword.

```
#import <Foundation/Foundation.h>

@interface Project : NSObject{
    @private NSString *log1;
    @protected NSString *log2;
}
```

```
@property(strong) NSString *name;

-(void)generateReport;
-(void)generateReportAndAddThisString:(NSString *)string
                 andThenAddThisDate:(NSDate *)date;
+(void)printTimeStamp;

@end
```

## Public Instance Variables

Public instance variables are available to the class they are coded in and all derived classes. In addition, other objects can reference public instance variables directly.

---

:::: **Note** I am discussing public instance variables here for the sake of completeness, but it is generally not accepted practice to use instance variables in this way. Instead, you should define properties to return any values that you want to make available to other objects.

---

To make an instance variable public, you must use the @public keyword.

```
#import <Foundation/Foundation.h>

@interface Project : NSObject{
    @private NSString *log1;
    @protected NSString *log2;
    @public NSString *log3;
}

@property(strong) NSString *name;

-(void)generateReport;
-(void)generateReportAndAddThisString:(NSString *)string
                 andThenAddThisDate:(NSDate *)date;
+(void)printTimeStamp;

@end
```

To use this object, you would need to use the **member of** operator, ->. The member of operator is a traditional C operation that you can use to reference a member of a structure that is referenced by a pointer. Here is an example of how you would do this:

```
#import <Foundation/Foundation.h>
#import "SpecialProject.h"

int main(int argc, const char * argv[]){
    @autoreleasepool {

        SpecialProject *sp = [[SpecialProject alloc]init];
        NSString *tempLog = sp->log3;
        NSLog(@"temp = %@", tempLog);

        return 0;
    }
}
```

# CHAPTER 19

# Categories

## Categories Defined

Categories are used to extend classes without using inheritance. When you use a category, you can add properties and methods to a class without declaring a super class.

To define a category, you need to add an interface and implementation. You can do this by adding new header and code files or you can add the categories right in the code file where you are working.

### Category Example

As an example, let's say that you want to take the Project class that you defined in Chapter 16 and add a constructor method that would initialize a new Project object and assign a name at the same time. You could add code like this right in the **main.m** file where you are coding.

The first thing you would do is add the interface.

```
#import <Foundation/Foundation.h>
#import "Project.h"

@interface Project(ProjectExtension)

@end

int main(int argc, const char * argv[]){
    @autoreleasepool {

        return 0;
    }
}
```

Category interfaces look similar to class interfaces, but they follow a slightly different format. These interfaces start with the @interface keyword and are followed by the original class name. Following the class name is the name of the category in parentheses.

You put forward declarations in the category interface. Since you want an initializer that sets the name for you, you would add something like this to your category interface:

```
#import <Foundation/Foundation.h>
#import "Project.h"

@interface Project(ProjectExtension)

-(id)initWithName:(NSString *)aName;

@end

int main(int argc, const char * argv[]){
    @autoreleasepool {

        return 0;
    }
}
```

The next step is to implement the new method, and to do that you must code the category implementation. Category implementations follow the same pattern as the category interface.

```
#import <Foundation/Foundation.h>
#import "Project.h"

@interface Project(ProjectExtension)

-(id)initWithName:(NSString *)aName;

@end

@implementation Project (ProjectExtension)

@end

int main(int argc, const char * argv[]){
    @autoreleasepool {

        return 0;
    }
}
```

Finally, you need to implement the new method just like you would for a class.

```
#import <Foundation/Foundation.h>
#import "Project.h"
```

```
@interface Project(ProjectExtension)

-(id)initWithName:(NSString *)aName;

@end

@implementation Project (ProjectExtension)

-(id)initWithName:(NSString *)aName{
    self = [super init];
    if (self) {
        self.name = aName;
    }

    return self;
}

@end

int main(int argc, const char * argv[]){
    @autoreleasepool {

        return 0;
    }
}
```

Now that you have the category set up, you can use this initializer to help you create and initialize new Project classes right inside the main function.

```
#import <Foundation/Foundation.h>
#import "Project.h"

@interface Project(ProjectExtension)

-(id)initWithName:(NSString *)aName;

@end

@implementation Project (ProjectExtension)

-(id)initWithName:(NSString *)aName{
    self = [super init];
    if (self) {
        self.name = aName;
    }

    return self;
}

@end
```

```
int main(int argc, const char * argv[]){
    @autoreleasepool {

        Project *p = [[Project alloc] initWithName:@"ThisNewProject"];
        NSLog(@"p.name = %@", p.name);

        return 0;
    }
}
```

If you were to build and run this project now, this would print out to the log:

```
p.name = ThisNewProject
```

# CHAPTER 20

# Blocks

## Blocks Defined

Blocks are a way to define a block of code that you will use at a later time. Blocks are a lot like methods or functions in that they can take parameters and return a value. Sometimes people refer to blocks as anonymous functions because they are functions that aren't attached to an entity.

One thing that sets blocks apart is that they are coded in the same scope as the rest of your program so you can add a block without a class definition. Blocks have some other properties that make them very useful. While blocks don't need to be attached to objects, blocks can be treated as objects. This means that you can code a set of blocks and then store them in a data collection.

Blocks also copy all the variable values that are in scope where the block is declared. This feature gives the block the ability to capture state and then use that state in the future, even if the original variables are out of scope when the block is executed.

### Defining Blocks

As an example, let's code a block that will take a float number as a parameter and then return a squared float result. Call the block squareThis. The first thing you need to do is to declare the block. This follows a similar pattern to declaring a datatype or an object, but with some differences that allow you to use the block's function-like behavior.

```
float (^squareThis)(float);
```

The block declaration starts with the float return type. This means that when you use this block, you will get a float number returned to you.

The next part of the block declaration is the name of the block squareThis proceeded by the caret (^) symbol. The entire name is enclosed in parentheses.

Finally, you have a list of parameter types enclosed in parentheses. If there is more than one parameter type, the list must be comma-separated. A semicolon ends the line of code.

## Assigning Blocks

You can use the assignment operator (= ) to assign a block of code to the block you just declared. When you assign the block code to the block variable, you will need to use the caret and declare variable names. You also need to include the code scoped with curly brackets.

```
squareThis = ^(float x){
    return x * x;
};
```

This block will take the number supplied, multiply the number by itself, and then return the result.

## Using Blocks

You can call the block like a function when you are ready to execute the code. Here is how you would use squareThis:

```
float result = squareThis(4);

NSLog(@"result = %f", result);
```

This will print out the following output to the console log:

```
result = 16.000000
```

## Copying Scoped Variables

Blocks copy the variable values of every variable that is currently in scope where the block is declared. This means that blocks can save the state of the variables around them to use at a later time when the block is executed, whether or not the variable is still in scope.

Here is an example of a block called multiplyThese that takes two numbers and multiplies them returning a float result. This block requires two parameters, and you will define and assign the block at the same time. Notice that that you also have a string defined near the multiplyThese block.

```
NSString *title = @"Multiply Block Execution";

float (^multiplyThese)(float, float) = ^(float x, float y){
    NSLog(title);

    return x * y;
};
```

Before returning the result, the multiplyThese block will print out the string value it captured from the context. To use this block, you would do this:

```
NSLog(@"multiplyThese(3,4) = %f", multiplyThese(3,4));
```

This will produce the following output:

```
Multiply Block Execution
multiplyThese(3,4) = 12.000000
```

# Blocks as Properties

Even though blocks don't require an entity like a class, you can use blocks to make objects more flexible. By adding a block to an object as a property, you can provide an interface to give clients a way to inject custom behavior into your objects.

## Block Forward Declaration

You can use blocks as properties since you treat blocks just like objects. To do this, you need to start in the class interface (either the public interface or the private class extension). Here is how you would add a customReport block to the Project class that you originally defined in Chapter 16:

```
#import <Foundation/Foundation.h>

@interface Project : NSObject{
    @private NSString *log1;
    @protected NSString *log2;
    @public NSString *log3;
}

@property(strong) NSString *name;
@property (copy) void (^makeCustomReport)(NSString *title);

-(void)generateReport;
-(void)generateReportAndAddThisString:(NSString *)string
                andThenAddThisDate:(NSDate *)date;
+(void)printTimeStamp;

@end
```

You need to use the copy property descriptor because you want the block and all its scoped variables to be copied and retained appropriately. The next thing you need to do as class authors is figure out when you want this block to execute, keeping in mind that you never know beforehand what code will be present in the block.

## Use Blocks in a Class

For this example, the generateReport method seems like a good place to do this. You need to go to the Project class implementation and find the generateReport method to add this block call.

```
#import "Project.h"

@implementation Project

-(void)generateReport{
    NSLog(@"This is a report!");
    self.makeCustomReport(@"Custom Project Report Title");
}

@end
```

If you look at the bold code above, you will see that using parameter blocks is just like using other blocks, except that you have the self keyword in place so that you can reference the block.

## Assigning Blocks

What is really powerful about this pattern is that you can set up a way to execute a behavior even if you don't know exactly what that behavior will be or if the behavior will change over time.

To get this to work, a client will need to assign the block and actually define that behavior for you. You can do this in the main function for your example.

```
Project *p =[[Project alloc]init];
p.makeCustomReport = ^(NSString* title){
    NSLog(@"%@", title);
    NSLog(@"This is a custom report requested by the author");
    NSLog(@"Say This");
    NSLog(@"Say That");
    NSLog(@"Say The Other Thing");
};
[p generateReport];
```

You need to send the generateReport message for your example; when you do, you will get this output:

```
This is a report!
Custom Project Report Title
This is a custom report requested by the author
Say This
Say That
Say The Other Thing
```

# CHAPTER 21

# Key-Value Coding

## Key-Value Coding Defined

Normally when you want to get or set property values in an object you use dot notation to get a reference to the property to change the value. However, with key-value coding you can store and retrieve property values indirectly using string keys. Applications that require archiving need this type of functionality so that apps can retrieve object data from archive files.

### Setting Property Values

You can use key-value coding to set property values. To set property values, you must use the setValue:forKey: message and provide the new property value and the NSString name of the property.

```
[p setValue:@"New Project" forKey:@"name"];
```

### Retrieving Property Values

To retrieve a property value using key-value coding, you can simply send the valueForKey message to the object. This message requires the property name in NSString format as a parameter. Here is how you would retrieve the name property value from a Project object:

```
NSString *retrievedName = [p valueForKey:@"name"];
```

This works for any type of object including data collection objects and custom objects. You could now print this value out to the log using the NSLog function.

```
NSLog(@"retrievedName = %@", retrievedName);
```

If you do this, you will get the following output, assuming the Project name was New Project:

```
retrievedName = New Project
```

# CHAPTER 22

▓ ▓ ▓

# Key-Value Observation

## Key-Value Observation Defined

One of the applications of key-value coding is implementing the observer pattern. The observer pattern is used when you want an object to get a notification when the state of another object changes. This pattern is implemented with key-value observation in Objective-C.

To see a clear example of key-value observation, you need at least two objects. One object will be observed while the other object will be observing. For this example, let's assume that you have two types of objects: a Project object and a Task object. Project objects maintain a list of Task objects. The project object needs to be notified when the state of a Task object changes (when the task is marked as complete, for example).

## Project and Task Object Graph

Let's go over this object graph before implementing key-value observation here. Project has been simplified for this example and I've added a Task class definition. The object graph will get set up in the main.m file.

Here is the interface for the Project class:

```
#import <Foundation/Foundation.h>
#import "Task.h"

@interface Project : NSObject

@property(strong) NSString *name;
@property(strong) NSMutableArray *listOfTasks;

-(void)generateReport;

@end
```

Here is the implementation for the Project class:

```
#import "Project.h"

@implementation Project

-(void)generateReport{
    NSLog(@"Report for %@ Project", self.name);
    [self.listOfTasks enumerateObjectsUsingBlock:^(id obj, NSUInteger idx,
BOOL *stop) {
        [obj generateReport];
    }];
}

@end
```

Here is the interface for the Task class:

```
#import <Foundation/Foundation.h>

@interface Task : NSObject

@property(strong) NSString *name;
@property(assign) BOOL done;

-(void)generateReport;

@end
```

Here is the implementation for the Task class:

```
#import "Task.h"

@implementation Task

-(void)generateReport{
    NSLog(@"Task %@ is %@", self.name, self.done ? @"DONE" : @"IN PROGRESS");
}

@end
```

Finally, you set up the object graph in main.m like this:

```
#import <Foundation/Foundation.h>
#import "Project.h"
```

```
int main(int argc, const char * argv[]){
    @autoreleasepool {

        Project *p = [[Project alloc]init];
        p.listOfTasks = [[NSMutableArray alloc]init];
        p.name = @"Cook Dinner";

        Task *t1 = [[Task alloc]init];
        t1.name = @"Choose Menu";
        [p.listOfTasks addObject:t1];

        Task *t2 = [[Task alloc]init];
        t2.name = @"Buy Groceries";
        [p.listOfTasks addObject:t2];

        Task *t3 = [[Task alloc]init];
        t3.name = @"Prepare Ingredients";
        [p.listOfTasks addObject:t3];

        Task *t4 = [[Task alloc]init];
        t4.name = @"Cook Food";
        [p.listOfTasks addObject:t4];

        return 0;
    }
}
```

This is going to give you a Project object named Cook Dinner with four tasks. Now you are ready to implement key-value observation.

# Implementing Key-Value Observation

You want Project objects to be notified when the state of their Task objects changes. So, if a Task object gets marked as complete, then the Project object will be notified. There are three steps to using key-value observation:

- Send the addObserver:forKeyPath:options:context: message to each object that is being observed.

- Override the method observeValueForKeyPath:ofObject:change:content: in the class definition of the object that is doing the observing.

- Override the dealloc method and remove the observer reference in the class definition of the object that is observing.

# Add the Observer

The easiest way to send this message to each Task that Project is responsible for is to use the listOfTasks enumeration method:

```
[p.listOfTasks enumerateObjectsUsingBlock:^(id obj, NSUInteger idx,
BOOL *stop) {
    [obj addObserver:p
            forKeyPath:@"done"
                options:NSKeyValueObservingOptionNew
                context:nil];
}];
```

This code can be located in the main.m file after all the Task objects have been added to the Project object. The first parameter after the AddObserver parameter descriptor is the object that will be observing. The next parameter is the key path, which is where you put the key for the property that you want to observe. Next you have some options that you can set; you can choose the NSKeyValueObservingOptionNew to keep track of new changes to the property value.

---

■ **Note**    You could have chosen NSKeyValueObservingOptionOld to get the previous values instead of the new values like you did above.

---

## Observing Value Changes

To receive a notification when a property value has changed, the object that is observing needs to override a method in the object's class definition. This is where you locate the code you need to respond to the change. Here is an example of how you would do this in the Project.m implementation file:

```
#import "Project.h"

@implementation Project

-(void)observeValueForKeyPath:(NSString *)keyPath
                    ofObject:(id)object
                      change:(NSDictionary *)change
                     context:(void *)context{

    if([keyPath isEqualToString:@"done"]){
        NSNumber *updatedStatus = [change objectForKey:@"new"];
        BOOL done = [updatedStatus boolValue];
```

```
        NSLog(@"Task '%@' is now %@", [object name], done ? @"DONE" :
@"IN PROGRESS");
    }
}

@end
```

---

▧ **Note**    The code above is added to the code that you added in the beginning of this chapter.

---

Whenever a Task object that you are watching changes its status, this method will execute. When this happens, you first test to make sure that the property you are expecting (done) is the property that changed. You need to do this because this method can be shared for all sorts of notifications.

In the next line of code, you pull out the NSNumber version of your property from the supplied NSDictionary changes before converting this to the BOOL type that you are expecting. Finally, you write out a report to the console log, reporting the updated status of the task.

Before you test this code, you need to clean up after yourself.

# De-Registering Observers

You need to make sure that the observer object goes through and stops observing each object since the observer object will soon be deleted. The place to perform this task is in the dealloc method. Every object has a dealloc method that executes before the object is removed from a program, so this is a good place to do this type of cleanup work.

Here is how you would code the dealloc method in the Project.m implementation file:

```
-(void)dealloc{
    [self.listOfTasks enumerateObjectsUsingBlock:^(id obj, NSUInteger idx,
BOOL *stop) {
        [obj removeObserver:self
                forKeyPath:@"done"];
    }];
}
```

This will enumerate through the listOfTasks array and remove the observer from each object.

# Testing the Observer

To test this, just change the done property in some of the Task objects. Each time you do this, you will see the report written out to the log. For example, let's say you did this in main.m:

```
t4.done  = YES;
t4.done  = NO;
t2.done = YES;
t1.done = NO;
```

Your Project object would be notified each time this state is changed, which would produce this output to the log:

```
Task 'Cook Food' is now DONE
Task 'Cook Food' is now IN PROGRESS
Task 'Buy Groceries' is now DONE
Task 'Choose Menu' is now IN PROGRESS
```

# CHAPTER 23

# Protocols

## Protocols Overview

Protocols are used to define a set of methods and properties independently of a class. Any class can adopt a protocol, which means that the class implements the properties and methods defined by the protocol. In effect, protocols define a contract that classes can agree to fulfill. When a class adopts a protocol, you can be confident that the class will have implemented the properties and methods in the protocol.

### Defining Protocols

To use protocols, you must start by defining the protocol. Use the @protocol keyword to start defining the protocol. You can simply include this in the same file as the class that the protocol is associated with or you can include the protocol in a separate header file. If you want to define a protocol for the Task class that you coded in the previous chapter, you could do this:

```
#import <Foundation/Foundation.h>
@class Task;

@protocol TaskDelegate <NSObject>

@optional

-(void)thisTask:(Task *)task statusHasChangedToThis:(BOOL)done;

@end

@interface Task : NSObject

@end
```

The protocol name follows the @protocol keyword and the word in the angle brackets is the protocol that you are inheriting. NSObject is the protocol that NSObject classes must conform to. Inheriting a protocol is like inheriting a class, but the implication now is that classes that adopt your protocol will be responsible for the methods that you define, in addition to the methods defined in the inherited protocol.

The protocol definition ends with the @end keyword. All the methods and properties between the @protocol and the @end are the methods that are required to be implemented when a class adopts this protocol.

---

▓ **Note**   You needed to use the @class keyword above because you referenced the Task class in the protocol before defining the class below. @class gives you a way of referencing a class without the interface.

---

## Optional and Required Methods and Properties

Protocol methods are required by default. However, you can specify methods to be optional. Optional methods are used when the functionality is present but not crucial. To mark methods as optional, use the @optional keyword. Every property and method that appears after the @optional keyword will be considered optional.

Use the @required key to mark methods and property as required. Every method and property that follows will be considered required.

## Adopting Protocols

You indicate that a class will adopt a protocol by including the protocol name in angle brackets after the superclass in the class interface. If a class adopts more than one protocol, then you must provide a comma-separated list of protocol names in the angle brackets.

If you want Project to adopt the TaskDelegate protocol, you would go to the Project interface and adopt the protocol, like this:

```
#import <Foundation/Foundation.h>
#import "Task.h"

@interface Project : NSObject<TaskDelegate>

@property(strong) NSString *name;
@property(strong) NSMutableArray *listOfTasks;

-(void)generateReport;

@end
```

Once you adopt the TaskDelegate protocol, you are agreeing to implement the TaskDelegate methods and properties. If you were to attempt to build your project right now, you would get a warning. The next thing you have to do is implement the methods defined in TaskDelegate.

# Implementing Protocol Methods

You implement protocol methods just as you would any other methods. You implement the protocol methods in the implementation of the class that adopted the protocol.

For this example, you would go to the Project class implementation and add this method:

```
#import "Project.h"

@implementation Project

-(void)thisTask:(Task *)task statusHasChangedToThis:(BOOL)done{
    NSLog(@"Task '%@' is now %@", task.name, done ? @"DONE" : @"IN
PROGRESS");
}

@end
```

You can't test this code yet because you still need to add code to give Task objects the ability to use this protocol. This is part of the Delegation design pattern that is covered in the next chapter.

# CHAPTER 24

# Delegation

## Delegation Defined

**Delegation** is a design pattern where one object asks another object for help. Protocols are an important part of **Delegation**, because protocols define how an object will be helped.

    **Delegation** works by defining a protocol that will list out all the methods and properties an object will need help with. Another object, known as the delegate, will provide the help needed by adopting and implementing the protocol methods. Objects ask for help by sending messages to their delegates.

### Defining Delegate Protocols

Let's say you want to implement **Delegation** for your object graph that includes the Project object and Task objects. In your object graph, your Task objects may need help from the Project object. For instance, when a Task status is marked as **Done**, the task may not know what to do next. The task could ask the Project for help if the Project was capable of acting as the Task's delegate.

    To make that happen, you would need to first define a protocol for Task that defined the ways that Task would need help. Luckily for you, you already did that in the previous chapter.

```
#import <Foundation/Foundation.h>
@class Task;

@protocol TaskDelegate <NSObject>

@optional

-(void)thisTask:(Task *)task statusHasChangedToThis:(BOOL)done;

@end
```

```
@interface Task : NSObject

@property(strong) NSString *name;
@property(assign) BOOL done;

-(void)generateReport;

@end
```

The protocol is called TaskDelegate (because you are using this to define how delegates can help you). thisTask:statusHasChangedToThis: is the method that delegates can use to help you.

## Delegate References

Objects that need help (Task objects in your example) need to maintain a reference to their delegate. You can reference the delegate by adding a property, usually called delegate, with the class type of id. The id class type must be followed by the protocol name in angle brackets indicating that the property can be any object as long as the protocol is implemented.

```
#import <Foundation/Foundation.h>
@class Task;

@protocol TaskDelegate <NSObject>

@optional

-(void)thisTask:(Task *)task statusHasChangedToThis:(BOOL)done;

@end

@interface Task : NSObject

@property(strong) NSString *name;
@property(assign) BOOL done;
@property(assign) id<TaskDelegate> delegate;

-(void)generateReport;

@end
```

You use the assign property descriptor because you don't want Task objects to have a strong relationship to the delegate object.

# Sending Messages to the Delegate

When Task objects need help, they can send messages to the delegate. Since you want this to happen when the Task status is changed, you can do this by writing a custom property accessor for the Task done property.

---

▓ **Note**    In Chapter 16, you declared properties and allowed them to be supported by automatically generated getters and setters. There are some situations where you want to code your own getters and setters.

---

You can send the message right in the Task done setter method.

```
#import "Task.h"

@implementation Task

-(void)generateReport{
    NSLog(@"Task %@ is %@", self.name, self.done ? @"DONE" : @"IN
PROGRESS");
}

BOOL _done;

-(void)setDone:(BOOL)done{
    _done = done;
    [self.delegate thisTask:self statusHasChangedToThis:done];
}

-(BOOL)done{
    return _done;
}

@end
```

In the setter, you can see that you are sending the message to the delegate. Your delegate can implement this method to respond to the event of the done property changing.

The other thing you may notice is that you have coded the getter as well. Even though you don't need to add any new code to the getter, you must manually implement both the getter and the setter when you decide to implement one or the other.

## Assigning the Delegate

The next step is to assign the delegate. In this example, this is something that can be done in the main.m file. You can do this by simply assigning the project to each task's delegate property.

```
Project *p = [[Project alloc]init];
p.listOfTasks = [[NSMutableArray alloc]init];
p.name = @"Cook Dinner";

Task *t1 = [[Task alloc]init];
t1.name = @"Choose Menu";
t1.delegate = p;
[p.listOfTasks addObject:t1];

Task *t2 = [[Task alloc]init];
t2.name = @"Buy Groceries";
[p.listOfTasks addObject:t2];
t2.delegate = p;

Task *t3 = [[Task alloc]init];
t3.name = @"Prepare Ingredients";
[p.listOfTasks addObject:t3];
t3.delegate = p;

Task *t4 = [[Task alloc]init];
t4.name = @"Cook Food";
[p.listOfTasks addObject:t4];
t4.delegate = p;
```

Now when you assign a different value to a task's done property, the Project delegate will be notified. In the last chapter, you already adopted the TaskDelegate protocol and implemented the protocol method -(void)thisTask:(Task *)task statusHasChangedToThis:(BOOL)done;.

When you set a done property on a Task object like this

```
t4.done = YES;
```

the protocol method you implemented in the Project implementation thisTask: statusHasChangedToThis: will execute. Remember, this is what you coded in the last chapter:

```
-(void)thisTask:(Task *)task statusHasChangedToThis:(BOOL)done{
    NSLog(@"Task '%@' is now %@", task.name, done ? @"DONE" : @"IN
PROGRESS");
}
```

This method will generate this output in the console log:

```
Task 'Cook Food' is now DONE
```

▦ ▦ ▦

# CHAPTER 25

# Singleton

## Singleton Defined

**Singleton** is a design pattern where you can have only one instance of a class. Usually, when you define a class, you expect to use many instances of the class. But in some designs this doesn't make sense.

For instance, an application may only need one reference to the file system (since there is only one file system). Or the app has a data model that should stay in sync and so you want to make sure you have only one instance of a class available.

To implement a **Singleton** pattern, you will need to create a special type of constructor and then only use this constructor to get a reference to the **Singleton** object.

### Singleton Interface

The first step is to code the interface. Let's assume that you are creating a class AppSingleton that will be your singleton. Here is how you would code the interface:

```
#import <Foundation/Foundation.h>

@interface AppSingleton : NSObject

+ (AppSingleton *)sharedInstance;

@end
```

What you have above is a class method that returns an instance of AppSingleton.

### Singleton Implementation

To implement this singleton, you need a static variable and the implementation of the class method sharedInstance that you defined in the interface.

```
#import "AppSingleton.h"

@implementation AppSingleton

static AppSingleton *singletonInstance = nil;

+ (AppSingleton *)sharedInstance{
    @synchronized(self){
        if (singletonInstance == nil)
            singletonInstance = [[self alloc] init];

        return(singletonInstance);
    }
}

@end
```

The static instance is an AppSingleton type named singletonInstance and you have it initially set to nil. In the sharedInstance method, you are testing the singletonInstance; if it is nil, then you will create a new instance. Either way you return this instance to the caller.

The code in this method is surrounded by the @synchronized(self) block. This is used to lock the code so that only one thread can use these lines of code at a time. This ensures that you only have one instance of this singleton even when you have more than one thread.

## Referencing Singletons

When you need a singleton object, you must use the method that returns the instance. This will be the method that you coded.

If you wanted to use the AppSingleton class, you would do this:

```
AppSingleton *ap = [AppSingleton sharedInstance];
```

This is used as in place of the alloc and init pattern normally used to create objects. You can do this from any class or file in your app, and each one will get the same instance of the class. The only caveat is that you must use the Singleton constructor; while you can still use alloc and init, doing so will break the pattern because these methods can still create more than one object while the constructor you created can only create one object.

# CHAPTER 26

# Error Handling

## Error Handling Defined

When programs encounter unexpected errors, they behave unexpectedly or stop working altogether. Ideally, programmers would find and fix all bugs before programs are used, but there are some situations were programmers don't have control of the entire situation. For instance, errors can happen when programs require resources like files or web sites that are no longer present.

The best practice in dealing with situations like this is to add error handling to a program. This means that when an error occurs, the program can recover or gracefully shutdown. NSError is the Foundation class that programmers use to deal with errors.

## NSError

One place where NSError is used frequently is when you are working with operations involving files. Many Foundation classes use NSError objects to help with error handling. The pattern is that you declare the NSError object and set it to nil before passing it by reference. Here is how this works with the NSString method that creates a string from the contents of a file:

```
NSError *error = nil;

NSString *file = @"/Users/Shared/array.txt";

NSString *content = [NSString stringWithContentsOfFile:file
                            encoding:NSStringEncodingConversionAllowLossy
                                      error:&error];
```

The & symbol that you see in front of the error parameter is called the **AddressOf** operator. This means that you are passing the memory address of the object and not a copy, so when the code in the method needs to modify the error object you will be able to see the results.

To check the error object, you would include code like this right after the message:

```
if(!error)
    NSLog(@"content = %@", content);
else
    NSLog(@"error = %@", error);
```

If there is no error, then do something with the content; otherwise, deal with the error. If this code is successful, then you would get this printed out to the log:

```
content = <?xml version="1.0" encoding="UTF-8"?>
<!DOCTYPE plist PUBLIC "-//Apple//DTD PLIST 1.0//EN" "http://www.apple.com/
DTDs/PropertyList-1.0.dtd">
<plist version="1.0">
<array>
        <string>A</string>
        <string>B</string>
        <string>C</string>
        <string>D</string>
</array>
</plist>
```

This file is something I had on my Mac, but the actual content doesn't matter. If you changed the filename to a file that didn't exist on my Mac, you would get the error message instead and it would look like this:

```
error = Error Domain=NSCocoaErrorDomain Code=260 "The file "arrayf.txt"
couldn't be opened because there is no such file." UserInfo=0x10010a8a0
{NSFilePath=/Users/Shared/arrayf.txt, NSUnderlyingError=0x10010a650 "The
operation couldn't be completed. No such file or directory"}
```

This is when you would use the app user interface to prompt the user for assistance.

# Try/Catch Statements

Try/catch statements are another way that you can try to catch errors. The idea is that you can identify areas of code that are error-prone and then wrap up these areas in a block, called the try block. You can also identify a block of code called the catch block that will execute if the code in the try block fails.

You can also set up a block of code called the finally block that will execute regardless of whether the try block fails or not. Let's try this by reading in an array file that only has four elements and then attempt to read a fifth element that would be out of bounds.

```
NSArray *array = [NSArray arrayWithContentsOfFile:file];

@try {
    NSString *fifthItem = [array objectAtIndex:4];
    NSLog(@"fifthItem = %@", fifthItem);
}
@catch (NSException *exception) {
    NSLog(@"exception = %@", exception);
}
@finally {
    NSLog(@"Moving on...");
}
```

If you execute this code, the try block would fail, and control would go to the catch block, and you would get a message printed out to the log:

```
exception = *** -[__NSArrayM objectAtIndex:]: index 4 beyond bounds [0 .. 3]
Moving on...
```

The text "Moving on..." appears because that is part of the finally block and will execute no matter what happens.

# CHAPTER 27

# Background Processing

## Background Processing Defined

When your program needs to do more than one thing at a time, you can use background processing. Background processing in Objective-C is done with a **Foundation** class called NSOperationQueue.

NSOperationQueue manages lists of operations and decides how to schedule the resources needed to run an operation. Operations are blocks of code. Operations can execute simultaneously or one at a time.

Let's say that you want to count to 10,000 while printing this out to the log. To do this, you would code something like the following:

```
for (int y=0; y<=10000; y++) {
    NSLog(@"y = %i", y);
}
```

This works fine. If you run this in an app, you will see a long list of y values printed out to the console log.

```
y = 0
...
y = 9998
y = 9999
y = 10000
```

Now, let's say you also want to count backwards from 20,000 to 0. If you just code another loop, then you would have to wait for the 10,000 count to complete before moving on to the 20,000 count. But if you use a background queue, you can do both tasks at once in potentially the same amount of time.

Here is how you could set this up using a background queue:

```
NSOperationQueue *background = [[NSOperationQueue alloc] init];
[background addOperationWithBlock:^{
    for (int i1=20000; i1>0; i1--) {
        NSLog(@"i1 = %i", i1);
    }
}];
```

```
for (int y=0; y<=10000; y++) {
    NSLog(@"y = %i", y);
}
```

You can create the queue with the `alloc` and `init` functions and then use the `addOperationWithBlock:` message to add a code block to the queue. If you run this code, you will get something like this printing out to the log:

```
i1 = 20000
y = 0
i1 = 19999
y = 1
i1 = 19998
y = 2
y = 3
i1 = 19997
i1 = 19996

. . .

y = 9997
i1 = 10001
y = 9998
y = 9999
i1 = 10000
i1 = 9999
y = 10000
```

## CHAPTER 28

# Object Archiving

## Object Archiving Defined

Saving a copy of your app's object graph to be used later on as a backup is called object archiving. Objective-C has classes that can help you archive your object graph. Each class that supports archiving must adopt the NSCoding protocol and implement two methods needed by the NSKeyedArchiver and NSKeyedUnarchiver classes.

## NSCoding

Each class that will support archiving must adopt the NSCoding protocol and implement the required methods. These methods will help the archivers to store the property values stored in the objects that need to be archived.

To adopt the NSCoding protocol, add the NSCoding protocol name in angle brackets to the class interface. Here is how you would do this for the Task class that you already coded:

```
#import <Foundation/Foundation.h>

@interface Task : NSObject<NSCoding>

@property(strong) NSString *name;
@property(assign) BOOL done;

-(void)generateReport;

@end
```

The syntax for the adopted protocol NSCoding is shown above in bold. Now you need to implement two protocol methods. The first method is called an encoder because it will be used to encode the property values into an archive file.

```
#import "Task.h"

@implementation Task
```

```
-(void)generateReport{
    NSLog(@"Task %@ is %@", self.name, self.done ? @"DONE" : @"IN PROGRESS");
}

-(void)encodeWithCoder:(NSCoder *)encoder {
    [encoder encodeObject:self.name forKey:@"namekey"];
    [encoder encodeBool:self.done forKey:@"donekey"];
}

@end
```

Each property that you want to save in the archive needs to have an encode message sent along with a key. Different data types require different messages. See Apple's NSCoding documentation for a complete listing of available methods. For instance, objects require the encodeObject:forKey: message while Boolean require the encodeBool:forKey: message.

Next, you need to implement the decoder method. This method is a type of constructor initializer that will add the property values to the object. As before, the significant methods are in bold.

```
#import "Task.h"

@implementation Task

-(void)generateReport{
    NSLog(@"Task %@ is %@", self.name, self.done ? @"DONE" : @"IN PROGRESS");
}

-(void)encodeWithCoder:(NSCoder *)encoder {
    [encoder encodeObject:self.name forKey:@"namekey"];
    [encoder encodeBool:self.done forKey:@"donekey"];
}

-(id)initWithCoder:(NSCoder *)decoder {
    self = [super init];
    if (self) {
        self.name = [decoder decodeObjectForKey:@"namekey"];
        self.done = [decoder decodeBoolForKey:@"donekey"];
    }
    return self;
}

@end
```

Each key and property in this method must match the ones in the encodeWithCoder: method. At this point, Task now supports NSCoding. To see an example, you also need to add NSCoding support to Project. Here is what you would do to the Project interface:

```
#import <Foundation/Foundation.h>
#import "Task.h"

@interface Project : NSObject<NSCoding>

@property(strong) NSString *name;
@property(strong) NSMutableArray *listOfTasks;

-(void)generateReport;

@end
```

Here is what you would do the Project implementation:

```
#import "Project.h"

@implementation Project

-(void)generateReport{
    NSLog(@"Report for %@ Project", self.name);
    [self.listOfTasks enumerateObjectsUsingBlock:^(id obj, NSUInteger idx,
BOOL *stop) {
        [obj generateReport];
    }];
}

-(void)encodeWithCoder:(NSCoder *)encoder {
    [encoder encodeObject:self.name forKey:@"namekey"];
    [encoder encodeObject:self.listOfTasks forKey:@"listOfTaskskey"];
}

-(id)initWithCoder:(NSCoder *)decoder {
    self = [super init];
    if (self) {
        self.name = [decoder decodeObjectForKey:@"namekey"];
        self.listOfTasks = [decoder decodeObjectForKey:@"listOfTaskskey"];
    }
    return self;
}

@end
```

# Using the Archiver

Assuming that you have an object graph already set up, it's easy to use the archiver. The class that you use is called NSKeyedArchiver and you just need to send the archiveRootObject:toFile: message. The two parameters are the filename that you want to use and the root object in the object graph. Your root object is the Project p object because you have only one p that contains many Task objects.

Let's assume that you still have the object graph created in Chapter 24 that listed out all the tasks for p. If you want to archive this, you could do this in the **main.m** file.

```
NSString *file = @"/Users/Shared/project.dat";
[NSKeyedArchiver archiveRootObject:p toFile:file];
```

This is will create a data file on your Mac. In the future, you could read in this file and use it to restore the object graph to your app.

```
NSString *file = @"/Users/Shared/project.dat";
Project *p = [NSKeyedUnarchiver unarchiveObjectWithFile:file];
[p generateReport];
```

Since you sent the generateReport message here, you would get a printout of the object graph in your console log.

```
Report for Cook Dinner Project
Task Choose Menu is IN PROGRESS
Task Buy Groceries is IN PROGRESS
Task Prepare Ingredients is IN PROGRESS
Task Cook Food is IN PROGRESS
```

# CHAPTER 29

# Web Services

## Web Services Defined

Many companies like Facebook and Twitter make their services available to users via web sites. Often these services are also available to developers to use in their apps; these are called web services. Web services are functions and content that reside on a web server that you can use via a well-defined set of rules called an API (Application Programming Interface).

The general pattern to working with web services is to formulate a request, send the request, receive the response, and then interpret the response. Objective-C comes with support for web services. To send requests and receive responses you can use the NSURLConnection class with the NSData class. To interpret, or parse, the response, you can use the NSJSONSerialization class.

---

**Note** JSON stands for JavaScript Object Notation and is used for data storage and transportation. Web services that are implemented as REST (Representational State Transfer) web services will provide JSON response data. The NSJSONSerialization class makes working with JSON easier in Objective-C.

---

## Bitly Example

Bitly is a good example of a web service that I like to use as a demonstration because it is pretty simple and provides a very clear function. Bitly will take a long URL (the string that you type into a web browser) and turn it into a short URL that is easier to type. I am going to use the bitly web service to showcase the NSURLConnection class.

---

**Note** To follow along with this recipe, you will need to create a free account with bit.ly and get your own API key and API username. Go to https://bit.ly to get your account if you wish to follow along with this example. In the examples, when I include [YOUR API LOGIN] or [YOUR API KEY] you will need to substitute the login and key that you obtained from bitly.

---

# Formulate Request String

When you work with a web service, you should use the documentation provided by the company that published the web service as a reference. This documentation will give you a string and parameters that you can use. You are going to use the string from the API documentation (http://api.bit.ly/shorten?version=2.0.1&longUrl=&login=&apiKey=&format=json) as a starting point along with the bitly login, bitly key, and a long URL as parameters to formulate your request string.

```
NSString *APILogin = @"[YOUR API LOGIN]";
NSString *APIKey = @"[YOUR API KEY]";
NSString *longURL = @"https://mobileappmastery.com";
NSString *requestString = [NSString stringWithFormat:@"http://api.bit.ly/
shorten?version=2.0.1&longUrl=%@&login=%@&apiKey=%@&format=json", longURL,
APILogin, APIKey];
```

# Create the Session and URL

You are going to need two objects: an NSURL object to represent the request URL that you are sending to the server and a NSURLSession object to do your web work for you.

```
NSURL *requestURL = [NSURL URLWithString:requestString];
NSURLSession *session = [NSURLSession sharedSession];
```

# Send and Receive the Response

You are going to use a block with the NSURLSession object to ask the web service to shorten the URL. Put all the code that you need to work with the response in the block that you send as a parameter. You are really doing two things at once with this method.

```
[[session dataTaskWithURL:requestURL
       completionHandler:^(NSData *data,
                                 NSURLResponse *response,
                                 NSError *error) {


       }] resume];

sleep(60);
```

You still need to fill in the block where you handle the response, but this will start the action. Notice that you need to put a sleep function in this code. The sleep function will stop new code from executing on the main thread for 60 seconds. You need this because the method you are using is going to execute on a background thread (this is the best practice when using web services). If you don't stop the command line app from finishing the web service, it won't have enough time to fetch the results for you.

# Parsing JSON

Inside the completion block, you can add the code used to interpret the response from the web server. Since you know that you are going to be working with JSON, you will use the NSJSONSerialization class. You need an NSError object here as well as the NSData object supplied by the block (this contains the data from the web service response).

```
[[session dataTaskWithURL:requestURL
        completionHandler:^(NSData *data,
                            NSURLResponse *response,
                            NSError *error) {

    NSError *e = nil;
    NSDictionary *bitlyJSON = [NSJSONSerialization
JSONObjectWithData:data

options:0

error:&e];

        }] resume];
```

This gives you all the JSON data organized in an NSDictionary collection. This dictionary can have other dictionaries, arrays, numbers, and strings located inside it. The next step is a process of going through all these returned objects to locate what you need. You also need to test for errors here.

```
[[session dataTaskWithURL:requestURL
        completionHandler:^(NSData *data,
                            NSURLResponse *response,
                            NSError *error) {

NSError *e = nil;
NSDictionary *bitlyJSON = [NSJSONSerialization JSONObjectWithData:data

options:0

error:&e];

if(!error){
    NSDictionary *results = [bitlyJSON objectForKey:@"results"];
    NSDictionary *resultsForLongURL = [results objectForKey:longURL];
    NSString *shortURL = [resultsForLongURL objectForKey:@"shortUrl"];
    NSLog(@"shortURL = %@", shortURL);
}
else
    NSLog(@"There was an error parsing the JSON");

        }] resume];
```

Once this is all set up, if you run your app, you will have retrieved the shortURL from the response and printed the following out to your console log:

```
shortURL = http://bit.ly/1fHrAsT
```

---

▓ **Note**   When you are parsing a web service response like this, you will need to investigate where the important data is by looking at the API documentation or viewing the string that is returned.

---

# Index

# Get the eBook for only $10!

Now you can take the weightless companion with you anywhere, anytime. Your purchase of this book entitles you to 3 electronic versions for only $10.

This Apress title will prove so indispensible that you'll want to carry it with you everywhere, which is why we are offering the eBook in 3 formats for only $10 if you have already purchased the print book.

Convenient and fully searchable, the PDF version enables you to easily find and copy code—or perform examples by quickly toggling between instructions and applications. The MOBI format is ideal for your Kindle, while the ePUB can be utilized on a variety of mobile devices.

Go to www.apress.com/promo/tendollars to purchase your companion eBook.